Behind the Facade

Behind the Facade

A MENTAL HEALTH MEMOIR

LAUREN BARTLESON

NEW DEGREE PRESS

BEHIND THE FACADE
A Mental Health Memoir

ISBN   979-8-88504-574-2   Paperback
        979-8-88504-899-6   Kindle Ebook
        979-8-88504-690-9   Ebook

To my dad, my hero.

How long for? Always.

DISCLAIMER

The stories shared within are my personal experiences and are in no way a substitute for professional advice or support. Please seek the advice of a mental health professional or another qualified health provider to discuss your unique circumstances.

If you or someone you know is experiencing suicidal thoughts, dial 988 to reach the Suicide Prevention Lifeline or text HOME to the Crisis Text Line at 741741. These services are free and confidential. If you are located outside the United States, call your local emergency line.

A QUICK NOTE

I had to step back in time to recall many of the moments and memories in the pages ahead. Some of those stories were previously hidden away, never to see the light of day. As I pulled them to the forefront of my mind, the timeline and details may have become fuzzy.

I purposefully chose not to use names in an effort to protect the privacy of those mentioned within. However, I couldn't get around sharing the identities of my mom, dad, brother, and husband; they previewed the book in advance and provided unconditional support for what's written here.

PREFACE

When I started writing this story, we were knee-deep in the COVID-19 pandemic, and I needed a project to distract me from the overwhelming dread I felt every time I picked up my phone. Like many, I was overly ambitious in that first year, thinking forced isolation would be the perfect time to write a book on top of making homemade sourdough, baking banana bread, and fermenting my own kombucha.

I knew I couldn't write alone, so I joined a virtual writer's group. After a rocky start, I set off to share the most personal tale I had ever written: my experience growing an online following. At its peak, the content documenting my weight loss journey reached over two hundred thousand people in 105 countries per month, and the extreme hate took a toll on my mental health. In one of our early sessions, I explained the book's premise to two fellow writers—a cautionary tale of sharing your life on social media, studded with tidbits of the chronic health issues my audience never saw.

After a brief silence, one of the women wondered aloud what caused me to gain weight in the first place. She asked a series of rhetorical questions, which led to a few of my own: *What got me to a place where I was so desperate to change? What caused me to alter my body so drastically that I was unrecognizable? Was I even remotely happy with my body as it was?*

When I tried to answer, my mind went blank. I was stunned into silence. How had I never thought about that before? I couldn't write about those pieces of the story because I didn't know. I had never thought about the root cause of my excessive weight. I often used the excuse that it was due to my underactive thyroid, but my endocrinologist told me in our most recent visit that my thyroid couldn't be the main factor. So what was it?

Feeling an overwhelming need to solve this puzzle, I recalled conversations with two doctors in unrelated fields: naturopathy and psychology. Within the span of a few weeks, they each told me I was dealing with trauma.

"But I haven't been to war, been in a life-altering accident, or experienced extreme violence," I replied.

I recalled a time in high school when I had an uncomfortable sexual experience, but I'd moved on years ago, so much so that I didn't mention it in either of those conversations. Regardless, both of the doctors insisted I was dealing with trauma. A lot of it.

As I dissected my past, I uncovered bits and pieces of life events that I had never truly processed before. In analyzing my childhood, which I had previously put into a black box and stored far, far away in the back of my mind, I realized the extreme bullying I experienced in middle school was considered trauma. I realized having two serious ex-boyfriends who hooked up with my friends, losing my dog, having chronic diseases, receiving hate comments online, and grieving someone who felt like a close friend were all considered trauma.

Woah.

Maybe they were right.

Maybe I *had* been dealing with trauma for the last twenty-plus years and didn't even realize.

In reliving these moments, it hit me: the story I wanted to tell—no, the story I *needed* to tell—was so much bigger than weight loss or even social media. It was about everyday trauma. It was a reminder to myself and anyone else who needed to hear it that the person on the other side of the screen is probably going through something that you may never see or know about. I viewed this as an opportunity to process and move on from my traumatic past, a chance to connect with others who may have gone through something similar. It was a way to reassure myself that my experiences were valid, and I was worthy of being loved, even if I was a little—or a lot—broken.

If you, too, are holding on to something or are tired of putting on a facade, living your life for other people, or feeling broken or overlooked by society's standards of trauma, I hope my story reminds you that you're not alone. I see you. I feel you. I am here with you.

Writing this book was a form of healing I didn't know I needed. I invite you to come on the emotional rollercoaster that I experienced while turning these life-altering realizations into what would become the pages you're currently holding in your hands. Thank you in advance for taking the time to read and support my work. I am immensely grateful.

1

SO IT BEGINS

The first time I noticed my weight was in fourth grade.

I was standing on the side of the playground next to a large, colorful square drawn in chalk on the pavement. A group of girls were playing foursquare, and I asked to play. Instead of welcoming me, they turned to each other, laughed, and collectively shook their heads no. They didn't say why, but I could tell by the disgust and annoyance on their faces and the way they immediately turned away snickering that it was something about me.

These were the four most popular girls in my class. They each wore girly dresses while I wore jeans and a frumpy sweatshirt. Their hair was long and wavy; by contrast, I had short, cropped hair, reminiscent of a boy's cut. They barely left each other's sides; I didn't have any close friends. They were skinny; I was big. I was different from them, and not in a good way.

Fast-forward to the following year: spring of fifth grade. Despite feeling like an outcast, I *loved* school, so much so that Monday was my favorite day of the week. I absolutely hated one class, though—gym class. I was a water baby through and through; I swam before I could crawl and felt more at home in water than on land. My dad and I often joked that I was built for water, not land; if I were running, it was because a bear—or in Monterey County's case, a mountain lion—was behind me.

I had been dreading mile day for weeks. It was a pass-fail assignment. If you finished in under twelve minutes, you passed; if you didn't, you failed. Even in elementary school, I did anything to avoid a bad grade on my report card, so I changed into my gym clothes—blood-red, knee-length shorts and a baggy gray t-shirt with our school's logo on it—and put on my sneakers before trudging behind my class down to the quarter-mile track, a dirt path surrounding a large grass field. After stretching, the class gathered at the start line, ready to make our way four times around the oval track.

Within seconds of hearing an ear-piercing whistle, I fell behind my classmates. Despite being the slowest of the bunch from the get-go, I gave it my all and was drenched in sweat and out of breath when I crossed the finish line at exactly twelve minutes. I didn't cross the line to a chorus of claps and whoops like everyone else did; instead, I came in to laughing and hushed whispers from my classmates. What should have been a proud moment—I ran a mile without dying!—was tainted with echoes of embarrassment and shame. To make it stop, I lied. I started limping, hoping to replace the sneers with sympathy.

"I think I hurt my leg," I told my gym teacher. "That's why I came in last."

Things only got worse in middle school. According to my mom, the public school district was seriously struggling in terms of money my sixth-grade year, the same year the twin towers were struck. They threatened no school buses, no extracurricular activities, no sports, no travel, and no school lunches, which my brother and I all but lived on during the school week. Along with hundreds of ornery families, my parents rushed to apply to a local private school, and my brother and I got in. We'd start the next fall; he in sixth grade, and me in seventh. Even though my new school was just ten minutes away in the heart of Carmel-by-the-Sea, my world flipped on its axis as I said goodbye to my friends, hello to a new school, and moved into a new house closer to town.

Our new school was split into two micro-campuses, one at the bottom of the hill where the kindergarten to fifth graders spent their days, and a separate building up a steep flight of stairs where middle school classes were held. The single-story, open-air building contained only four classrooms with lockers along the corridor.

At first, I loved going to my locker. It gave me a chance to connect with a girl in my grade who had quickly become a close friend, but a few weeks into the school year, it became the place I dreaded most. My friend started dating the most popular boy in the year below us, who, by default, became part of my life. Instead of becoming allies connected by our mutual friend, the boy's mission became to torment me.

The lockers went from being a welcome break in between classes to my personal hell. Every time he and I crossed paths in the hallway, he would purposefully bump into me, show his tight-lipped smile, and stop to call me names. It didn't matter if he was on his own, with my friend, or surrounded by his younger friends;

every hour on the hour, as we switched our books and replenished our backpacks, he would stop by my locker to share a new "joke."

Before I could get to my locker in the morning, he'd block my path, announcing to anyone nearby that, "The fat pig has arrived." Like clockwork, my hands clammed up and my cheeks heated within seconds. As soon as I picked up my books, I ran to homeroom, my eyes welling with tears.

As I walked to my locker after second period, I saw him waiting for me.

"Here she is," he stated proudly. "The fat whale," insinuating that, like the large sea creature, I had a thick layer of blubber surrounding my muscles and organs. Unlike the Humpback whales we often saw in Monterey Bay, my extra layer didn't keep me warm; my fat brought me unwanted attention and made me stand out from the other kids.

Each time I heard one of his insults, I became a little smaller. My shoulders dropped an inch and my eyes darted to the ground, avoiding looking at his face for fear of breaking down in the middle of the hallway. Rather than being mad at him, I was mad at myself, frustrated I couldn't change my body. Without saying anything, I stepped around him and put all of my effort and energy into opening my locker, coaching myself step-by-step through the process:

Spin the dial clockwise three full times.
Find the first number.
Spin the dial counter-clockwise.
Repeat twice.
Open the locker and get my stuff.

Close the locker, insert the lock, and walk away.
Don't look up.
Don't look up.
Don't look up.

As soon as I walked into my next classroom, I collapsed into my assigned desk, a safe haven where I could just *be* for the next fifty minutes. When the bell rang to signal the end of class, my body immediately tensed in anticipation. I struggled to decide whether I should hurry so I could say hi to my friend in between classes or take my time packing my backpack, carefully placing one book in my bag at a time rather than haphazardly throwing them all in at once. Most times, I opted for the latter, hoping if I gave him enough time, he wouldn't be at my locker waiting for me.

To my utter disappointment, they were always both there: my least favorite person and my close friend. As he told me how much I resembled a rhino, I silently repeated the same instructions—*open lock, grab Lunchables, close lock*—doing everything in my power to stand tall and avoid meeting his gaze before walking to the other side of the building to eat lunch.

Despite standing next to me for at least one insult per day, not once did my friend stand up for me. I never confronted her, either; I wanted a best friend and was afraid she would choose him over me if I said anything. When I looked at her in desperation, hoping my watery eyes would convince her to tell him to stop, she'd just laugh and say, "He's just joking. Let it go." To me, it wasn't a joke. His words seeped deep into my bones, becoming my truth.

Sometimes, especially toward the end of the day, he would spice it up and make fun of my uniform, my hair, my face, or anything else he could to get a rise out of me. No matter what he said, he would linger for a minute, the corners of his mouth lifting as he watched me squirm, trying—and failing—to hide my shame and embarrassment, before turning around to find his friends and laughing at my misery.

After school, I had only one way to get to my mom's car in the pick-up line, by walking right past his locker, where he gathered with a large group of friends, including my brother.

"Let's go," I'd tell my brother. "Mom's waiting."

"Tell her I'll be right there," he'd reply coolly, trying to impress his friends.

As I hurried past the group, the bully couldn't help but add, "See ya tomorrow, elephant." No one—not even my brother—responded.

By the time I got into the car at the end of the day, I all but collapsed in the front seat, mentally exhausted from battling a one-sided war.

"How was school?" my mom asked innocently, unaware of what I had been through over the past seven hours.

"Good," I replied before telling her about my classes. "We read more Shakespeare in English."

I never told my mom—or any adult, for that matter—what he said. I also never confronted my friend about not standing up for me, and I didn't ask my brother to stick up for me, either. I didn't want to cause a scene.

Without fail, the bully and I went through the same routine every day. Sometimes he would switch up the animal, calling me a hippo instead of an elephant, but that was the extent of it. I tried not to let it get to me, but how could it not? I tried not to give him the satisfaction of a reply, but that was easier said than done. I pretended not to hear him, but I did—every time, every word.

As soon as I got home from swim practice, I'd run upstairs and turn on the computer, eager to log into Myspace and see if anyone posted on my wall or liked one of my posts. The internet was a safe place; somewhere he couldn't reach me. Until it wasn't. One evening, I received a notification for a new comment. It wasn't from one of my internet friends, as I expected; it was from *him*.

I froze as I read a version of the same comment I'd heard so many times in person: him making fun of my body, calling me another animal. This time, though, I wasn't the only one who could see it. Every single one of my friends could. The realization sent me into an immediate panic. *Do I delete the post? Do I keep it to show I'm cool enough to receive posts on my wall, especially from a boy?* I opted to keep it, not realizing that my parents could see his comment, too.

Later that week, I got called into the principal's office.

"What's going on?" I asked the receptionist on our way to the office. It was rare I was called out of class, and I couldn't think of anything I had done wrong. As we walked into the room, I stopped mid-step, my eyes looking around the room in horror. My mom was there, along with the boy and his parents. *This can't be good*, I thought.

"Your mom showed us what he said to you on Myspace," the principal said.

Within seconds, my face warmed in embarrassment. I hadn't told anyone for a reason; I didn't want *this*—unwanted attention and awkwardness—to happen. When the principal told the boy to apologize, he simply mumbled, "Sorry," before crossing his arms and rolling his eyes.

"Louder," his mom said. "Like you mean it."

"SORRY" he said louder, his voice booming with anger at being forced to say something he didn't mean.

After the insincere apology, the principal told him he was suspended for his actions and assured me it wouldn't happen again. My mom thanked her and guided me out to the car. No way was I going back to class after *that* embarrassment.

As soon as we got in the car, I curled up into as small of a ball as possible.

"Promise you won't tell Dad or anyone else?" I begged, embarrassed that I just walked out of the principal's office and got the most popular boy suspended from school.

"I promise."

At the next family gathering, my aunt gave me a hug and apologized for what was happening at school.

"What are you talking about?" I asked curiously.

"Well that boy...you know," my aunt said hesitantly.

Rage poured through my veins, my eyes narrowing as I found my mom across the room. She'd *promised* she wouldn't tell anyone and now my entire family knew about it?

I'll never trust her again, I promised myself in my twelve-year-old angst.

Despite the school—and seemingly our whole town— knowing about the bullying, he continued to harass me multiple times per day as soon as he came back from his three-day suspension. *Pig, rhino, elephant. Pig, rhino, elephant. Pig, rhino, elephant.* Day in and day out, he wore me down until I believed in my core that I really was a fat whale.

All I could do was count down the days until the end of the school year, knowing I would be going to high school while he stayed to finish eighth grade. For the first time in two years, I would be able to go a full day without his name-calling.

2
THE POWER OF
PEER PRESSURE

"Isn't that where Clint Eastwood was mayor?"

That's the reply I typically get when I tell people I grew up in Carmel, a tourist town on California's Central Coast, two hours south of San Francisco. For the first half of my childhood, I lived twelve miles away in Carmel Valley Village before moving to the mouth of the valley, just outside of Carmel-by-the-Sea, the renowned town known for its historic Spanish mission, storybook-like cottages, and high-end art galleries.

In light of the bullying, my parents decided to transfer me to the public high school. After being absent for two years, I wasn't sure where I belonged. I took AP classes but didn't hang out with the brainiacs. I was swim captain but didn't associate with the jocks. Each time I'd befriend someone new, I'd undoubtedly make my way back to my friend group from sixth grade, jumping back in like nothing had changed.

An average day in high school started early: swim practice for the club team at 6 a.m. before going straight to school and then back to practice at 3:00 p.m.—either basketball, water polo, or the school's swim team, depending on the year and season. On weekends, vacations, and practice-free afternoons, I'd work one of many jobs: lifeguarding in my classic red swimsuit, selling candles at a local candle store, pulling shots as a barista, or ringing up orders in an upscale boutique.

Looking back, I was likely running a hundred miles an hour to distract myself from the emotions I was feeling deep inside. By this point, the damage of extreme bullying had been done. I believed I was unworthy, a waste of space, a fat pig. Instead of confronting these emotions, I pushed them down further and further, donning a mask, and becoming who I assumed other people—my parents, perhaps—wanted me to be: an overachiever.

When I wasn't at practice or working, I hung out with friends. In my absence, my three closest friends had veered toward a lifestyle I wasn't sure I wanted to live. They dabbled in alcohol and drugs, their weekends filled with drunk driving, raves, and parties. Despite being hesitant, I partook anyway, torn between wanting to feel part of the group and staying loyal to my family's expectations of avoiding illegal substances.

It started spiraling out of control my sophomore year when one of our friends, a girl a year older than the rest of us, got her license. With this freedom, we could finally stop relying on our parents for rides and go anywhere, anytime, without restriction. Our evening and weekend outings tended to revolve around parties to meet college guys, typically via a connection that one of the other girls had. More often than not, I'd get in the car, not knowing where we were going but grateful to feel included.

One night, we arrived at an apartment complex in Monterey, a short drive from Carmel. I hadn't been to that particular building or met the person whose apartment it was before, but I trusted my friends and followed them up the stairs through a chipped front door. The room was bare; other than a few boxes, a small wooden coffee table and lamp sat in one corner of the room, and that was it.

While a group of guys I had never met went to the back room, my friends and I gravitated to a corner of the living room to sit on the floor and take swigs out of a handle of cheap vodka. When the bottle got to me, I passed it to the next person, laughing off the peer pressure by saying, "Not this time; maybe the next round." It was rare I didn't participate.

We'd been in the apartment for less than an hour when my friends started pressuring me to hook up with the guy who lived in the apartment. I barely knew his name, much less anything about him other than the fact that he had an infant in the next room. We had shaken hands and introduced ourselves when I walked in the door, but that was it.

I told them I wasn't comfortable, but my friends kept pushing and pushing, encouraging me to "just get it over with." I was the only one who hadn't slept with anyone and they "wanted me to officially become one of them."

"We talked to him beforehand and he's up for it," my friend who had met him before promised.

"It's not like anyone else will want you," another added.

"Now's your shot," the third chimed in.

After saying no time and time again, the pressure got to me. I convinced myself that they were right. *Sex isn't special. No one will want me. Might as well get it out of the way. Plus, it'll get them off my fucking back.* So when one of them quite literally pushed me into the room to "do it" with this older guy, I let it happen. His baby was watching us from her crib. Because we didn't kiss, talk, or touch, it was over in minutes, though it felt like hours. Even though a wall stood between me and my friends, it felt like all eyes were on me.

A few minutes later, I walked out to smiles and cheers. "Good job!" one of my friends said loudly, like losing your virginity to someone you'd never met was a good thing, an accomplishment. I rejoined the circle, holding in tears of pain, discomfort, frustration, and, most of all, embarrassment. I wanted to leave but couldn't. As usual, I was at the mercy of someone else's time and ride.

To this day, I can't tell you the guy's last name or where he lived. I have no recollection of what he looked like, only a vivid snapshot of where I was standing in relation to the crib and a memory of my three friends and I sitting on the floor in a circle. Instead of feeling betrayed, like my friends took something from me that I'd never be able to get back, I was proud to officially be one of them.

Over the summer and into my junior year, I slowly drifted away from these friends and immersed myself in a group of girls from class who were kind, supportive, and straight-edge—the total opposite of my previous friend group. My Friday evenings went from getting drunk at a random person's apartment to staying in and eating pizza, dressing up for movie premieres, or wandering the mall. The girls had been close friends for years, and although they let me in, I still felt like the outsider. I kept them at arm's length, believing it would stay that way regardless of how many times each girl invited me to hang out at their home.

After a few months, I befriended a girl in my grade who had recently relocated to Carmel. With her dark brown, perfectly curled hair and pristine makeup, she was the epitome of a Southern Belle, her Texas roots shining through in her walk, voice, and mannerisms. We hit it off immediately. She was the best of all my friendships. We could spend a Friday night lounging at home in pajamas watching a movie, or we could go out on the town, partying and having fun. We talked about school and boys and sports and supported each other in our various extracurricular activities and passions. We'd drive down to the beach in her Mini Cooper, windows down, hair blowing in the wind, feeling like the world was our oyster. I finally had a friend with whom I didn't have to pretend to be someone I wasn't. I was just me— the brainiac, jock, and outsider—and she accepted me for each of those things. In hindsight, she was my first real friend; the first person I could truly be myself with.

Six months into our friendship, things turned sour. I shouldn't have been surprised when she started dating my brother, but I was. Unlike me, my brother was popular. Our house was walking distance from the high school so it became the after-school hangout spot, and our den would fill with dozens of his friends and classmates. On our way into the house, my friend and I would often stop by and say hi, trying to weasel ourselves into the conversation. Before long, she became part of the crowd while I remained on the sidelines watching.

In the blink of an eye, she and my brother became an inseparable pair while I remained the third wheel, receiving a brushed-off, "Want to join?" at the last minute instead of the first invite. Feeling left out, I made my way back to my initial friend group—the girls who I had known in middle school—with my tail between my legs. I wanted to feel wanted by someone, *anyone,* and this group was safe. They welcomed me back with open arms, like nothing had ever changed.

By this time, we were heading into our senior year of high school. Despite the trauma they put me through in the apartment on that dreadful night two years earlier, I was thankful to have a group to sit with at lunch and to have plans with on practice-free afternoons. I had known one of these girls since fourth grade, and she had become like family, even coming on week-long family vacations with my parents and brother. She was a serial dater who was, at the time, with someone a few years older than us.

"He has this friend," she told me over lunch one day. "You should date him so we can hang out as a foursome over lunch and after school. Plus, it's not like anyone else would date you," she added, throwing a dart straight into my weak spot yet again. I impulsively brought my right hand to my mouth to gnaw at my already-short nails, thinking of how to respond.

"I'm in," I told her begrudgingly. Despite her irritatingly smug smile and the laughter bubbling beneath her comments, I couldn't bear to disappoint her.

The foursome was instant and convenient. Within weeks, my new boyfriend and I fell into the high school kind of love where you can't do anything without the other person. Like me, he seemed to feel like no one else would want him, which made us an even stronger couple. Unlike me, he was stoned twenty-four-seven, which I hated at first but began to tolerate as the months went on. Due to his age, he was banned from prom and other school events, so I missed out on those quintessential high school experiences in lieu of spending time with him. I toyed with the idea of going alone, but when I brought it up, he convinced me not to. My time, body, and choice in activities were his and his alone.

One day, our boyfriends met me and my friend at the high school parking lot so we could get lunch. The four of us piled into my green Infiniti that drove more like a boat than a car. My friend and her boyfriend sat in the backseat while I drove, my boyfriend sitting in the passenger seat beside me. I started driving the five minutes to Safeway, our default for when we weren't sure where else to eat. I wore a babydoll tank top from Forever21 that I had been looking forward to wearing since I bought it a few weeks prior. It had thick light pink straps with a sheer material over the chest, the bottom covered in baby pink roses; paired with brand jeans, it was a feminine and girly outfit that I felt wildly confident in... until I glanced down at my phone at a stop light, seeing a notification for a text message flash up on the screen.

Look at what Lauren's wearing lol, the notification read, followed by a second message about how embarrassing my shirt was.

I looked in the rear-view mirror, seeing a smirk on my friend's face as she looked over at her boyfriend, waiting for his response. Little did she know, she accidentally sent the text to me, not him.

My right hand slipped out of my boyfriend's grasp, suddenly clammy and sticky. I stepped on the gas, thanking the light for finally turning green. *The sooner we get to Safeway,* I thought, *the sooner I can get the hell out of this car and away from her.*

In the two minutes it took to get to the parking lot, I convinced myself to leave her and her boyfriend at Safeway, a form of revenge for the embarrassment she unknowingly put me through. *Take that,* I imagined saying to her after the fact.

When we parked, I got out of the car and, acting like nothing happened, followed her into the grocery store, the whole time scheming how to leave her and her boyfriend behind without being too abrupt or awkward. I hadn't told my boyfriend what happened, so he couldn't help me plan an escape. I considered leaving all three of them there, but each time I pulled out my car keys, I chickened out, preconceived guilt keeping me from playing out the scenario in my mind.

Before I knew it, the four of us were back in the car, buckling our seatbelts, and driving back to campus. Rather than being frustrated with my friend, I was disappointed in myself for not following through.

Why couldn't I, for once, stand up for myself without the fear of letting someone else down in the process?

She never apologized; never acknowledged the text although I'm sure she realized what happened within seconds, if not minutes. Instead, she easily excused herself by acting like it never happened—but it did. Her snide smile in the rearview mirror, the babydoll tank top, and the message notification were instantly burned in my mind.

Despite the anger, frustration, and resentment, I never said anything either. Every time I saw her in the hallways, at a friend's house, or at a party, I had that nagging thought: *What does she* really *think of me?* The fear of losing a friend scared me more than the sting of a text message, so when I saw her, I plastered on a smile, gave her a side hug, and said "How's it going?" instead. To anyone else, it looked like our friendship was better than ever. In reality, it was anything but.

3

FIRST HEARTBREAK

I met my college boyfriend when I was drunk.

We were both freshmen at California Polytechnic State University, San Luis Obispo, just two hours south of my hometown. Between Greek life, living in the dorms, and business classes, I had a solid group of friends within weeks. My new friends and I typically spent Friday and Saturday nights attending whichever house party we could weasel our way into. At one of these parties I caught the eye of a tall guy wearing a gray t-shirt, plaid chino shorts, and a bright turquoise hat covering his unruly brown hair.

I made my way over to where he stood, tipsy enough to make the first move.

"Hey," I said with a flirty tone and a smile. "What year are you?"

"Freshman, you?"

"Same," I replied. "I'm studying business and have my heart set on marketing. What's your major?"

"Mechanical engineering," he said distractedly, glancing over my shoulder, perhaps looking for a friend or someone else to talk with.

Well, this is awkward, I thought. *He obviously doesn't want to talk to me. Also, get a grip, Lauren. People don't want to talk about school at a party.*

"I'm going to grab a drink," I said, excusing myself. "See you later."

After a few shots, I meandered outside to grab some air. As soon as I stepped onto the porch, I clumsily collapsed onto the stairs, instantly captivated by a group of guys playing beer pong in the front yard.

"Mind if I sit?" When I looked up, my breath hitched as his husky blue eyes locked on mine. The alcohol loosened both of us up, and our conversation flowed more easily than it had when we were nearly sober. Over the next few minutes, perhaps hours, I learned that, other than our brown curls, we had little in common. He was from Southern California; I was proud of my NorCal roots. He was quiet and reserved while I was loud and outgoing, trying to be someone I wasn't. He was a jock—football captain—and, although I was a regionally-ranked swimmer, I didn't consider myself worthy of a star athlete. Even so, we hit it off right away, becoming inseparable from the moment he asked to walk me home.

After a few months, we embarked on our first road trip together. The plan was to head two and a half hours north to visit my family in Carmel before turning around and driving eight hours south to his hometown, a suburb of San Diego, so I could meet his family. From there, we'd head back to school together.

When we got to Carmel, an acquaintance from high school stopped by for a quick hello. The minute she walked in the door, my not-quite-boyfriend looked over at me, eyebrows raised. My friend's long brown hair, caked-on makeup, and expensive outfit made her look like a supermodel.

He looked over at me, his eyes raised in surprise. He asked through his body language, "*This* is the kind of girl you hung out with in high school?"

"Yep," I silently replied, my eyes darting away from his. I didn't want to be with someone who eyed other women, but at the same time, I was already falling for him and couldn't imagine not being together. I tried but failed to let it go.

That night, we met up with three of my close friends at a local hookah bar, two of which had pushed me into the room the night I lost my virginity. I hadn't forgiven them, but I hadn't cut off our friendship either. In the three years since, things had continued as if nothing had happened.

"Lauren! Lauren! Wake up! Are you okay?" one of my friends was violently shaking my right arm, willing me to wake up.

"What happened?" I asked groggily. I looked up to see a swarm of paramedics surrounding me and a group of firemen a few feet away.

"I don't know," she replied, her blue eyes staring at me with concern. "You were shaking and drool was coming out of your mouth, like you were having a seizure. What happened?"

I shook my head, trying to recall any details from the last few moments. My mind was black, completely empty.

"I have no idea," I replied, looking around at my friends and the guy I was seeing, who was sitting frozen in his chair, for help.

"Take it easy," one of the paramedics said sharply as I tried to sit up straight.

"We called your parents," my friend told me. "We weren't sure what to do."

"We need to take you to the hospital," the paramedic said somewhat urgently. "Let's get you over to the ambulance."

"Can we please wait until my parents get here?" I asked, unsure of whether to go. My dad would know. I needed him here.

Thankfully, my parents showed up a couple of minutes later, a perk of living a ten-minute drive from Monterey. My dad, a former paramedic and surgeon, hopped out of the car and strode over to the ambulance.

"Hi, Dad," I said to him, shock and fear making my voice teeter. "I'm so happy you're here." I wouldn't want anyone else in the world with me—or advocating for me—in a time like this.

He introduced himself to the paramedics, immediately taking control of the situation.

"Thank you for helping my daughter," he said calmly. I couldn't understand how my dad and the emergency responders were all so calm during a time like this. I was more on par with my mom's crisis response: pacing in panic and talking a million miles an hour while trying to figure out what happened.

"We don't need to take her to the hospital right away," my dad said firmly. "I'm familiar with petit mal seizures and how to care for a patient who may have had one."

"We strongly recommend she goes to the hospital, if only to get a checkup," the paramedic countered.

"I'll keep a close eye on her," he promised.

My dad guided me to the car, holding my back firmly, on standby to catch me if I lost balance or had another seizure.

Over the next two days, my dad watched me like a hawk. My quasi-boyfriend, on the other hand, looked like a deer in the headlights anytime I so much as adjusted while lying down. I couldn't help but laugh at how different they were. The cause of the seizure was never discovered, but I remained on edge that something similar would happen again.

After a few days with no follow-up incidents, we packed up to head to San Diego as planned. In the spur of the moment, my girlfriends from the hookah bar decided to join us for the road trip. One of the girls had a friend who lived near Los Angeles, so we made the five-hour trek to their house, planning to spend the night partying before finishing the drive the next day.

I went to bed earlier than the others, exhausted from the day's drive and the booze that filled my system. A couple hours later, I woke up to use the bathroom. In my disoriented state, I stumbled out of the bedroom straight into the guy I was seeing, who was lip-locked with a tall blonde, her back against the wall. It could only be one person: one of my close girlfriends, the one who had shown such concern after my seizure. I froze in shock, completely caught off guard at the scene unfolding in front of me.

We weren't together, I convinced myself, zeroing in on him.

Despite being inseparable for months, he and I hadn't had the boyfriend-girlfriend conversation yet, so I gave him the benefit of the doubt. Even so, my mind spiraled with what-ifs, wondering why he kissed my closest friend instead of me. *Maybe I wasn't his type. Maybe I wasn't a good kisser. Maybe I was too fat.* Before either of them could see me, I sulked away, backing quietly into the shadows. I got back in bed, pulled the covers over my head, and pretended like nothing happened. I forgot to use the bathroom.

The next afternoon, once our hangovers wore off and our headaches subsided, we hit the road for the three-hour drive to San Diego. I didn't say a word to either of them—the guy I was already starting to fall for and one of my oldest friends—on the trip; instead, I gave them both the cold shoulder. I turned the music up as loudly as I could manage, focusing all of my energy on the road. When the image of them together the night before flashed into my mind, I gripped the steering wheel as tightly as I possibly could, squeezing until both sets of knuckles turned bright white. Although I wanted nothing more than to turn around and go home, I kept on driving. I had a destination and wouldn't turn around until I got there.

By the time we arrived, the sun had set. During the drive, the sky changed from a blend of oranges and pinks to black illuminated by the city lights, a welcome distraction from my swirling thoughts. We dropped my whatever-he-was off at his parents' house, turned around, and drove straight back to Carmel in the dead of night. Too angry and tired to drive, I let my friend, the one who kissed the guy I was seeing, take the driver's seat. She illegally weaved in and out of the carpool lane, driving one hundred miles an hour, well over the sixty-five-mile-per-hour speed limit. I sat in the passenger seat, alternating between hanging on for dear life and staring blankly out the window, deciding what to do.

What happens to our friendship? I wondered as I glanced over at my close friend.

What happens to our relationship? I asked myself, thinking about the guy I had invested so much time and energy into over the previous three months.

I couldn't answer either question. My emotions were all over the place, ping-ponging between anger, disappointment, confusion, and, most of all, heartbreak. I'd trusted both of them and they betrayed me.

As soon as we got home, my friends got in their cars and drove away. I never contacted any of them, eager to leave our friendship behind after the second round of betrayal from the same group. I often thought about my closest friend, the one who kissed my almost-boyfriend, but I was lost in so much resentment that I ghosted her, unable to face what happened. A few years later, she offered an olive branch, which I took, but our friendship was never the same.

The guy, on the other hand, was forgiven in a heartbeat. He knew something was off once I gave him the cold shoulder and refused to stay in San Diego. He called groveling in the morning, asking for forgiveness for "whatever I did wrong." I couldn't say what he did aloud, in fear of breaking my own heart. Instead, I forgave him without fanfare.

There was no question about whether we would stay together or not. I reveled in his attention, and I needed his affection, whether it was sincere or not. When we agreed to meet at my dorm back in San Luis Obispo, we instantly fell back into our attached-at-the-hip routine, going out together like nothing ever happened. A few weeks later, we made our relationship official.

Over the next three years, my boyfriend threw countless subtle hints my way that, even though he loved me, I was too big, too heavy, too much. Although he never said these things to my face, I read between the lines by the way he refused to hold my hand in public, the way he eyed other women, and the way he reacted to my body in bed. In my mind, I believed it was my fault; that he was ashamed of who I was and what I looked like.

As our college careers came to an end, we decided to take a break. He was busy with his final quarter and needed to focus on school while I was graduating early and wanted to enjoy the two international trips I had planned. In a few short months, I would be moving to San Jose to pursue my dream of working in marketing at a tech company in Silicon Valley and wanted to soak up as much of my free time as I could. Plus, his behavior was becoming erratic, making me more and more uncomfortable as the days went on. More than once during our senior year, I caught him drinking whiskey before noon on a school day, trying to "ease the stress."

One evening, we were in my apartment arguing about something minor. I was standing by the door to my balcony, looking out at the trees while he sat on my leather couch across the room, my twin-sized bed nestled between us. Out of the corner of my eye, I saw something flying across the room toward me. I covered my ears, my classic response when I'm scared, and ducked; the television remote just barely missed my head. Thankfully, it didn't break the glass door behind me.

"What the hell?" I asked, caught off guard.

"Get out of my apartment—now," I stated. I purposefully didn't raise my voice or yell, worried it would set him off again.

"I'm sorry," he said, pleading. "I didn't mean to. It was an accident."

"Get. Out." I said again, this time more firmly.

"You're being dramatic," he told me. "It was an accident. I was just frustrated."

I planted my feet and crossed my arms in front of me, refusing to back down.

"I'm not going to ask you again," I said, louder than before.

He turned toward the door in slow motion, proceeding to slouch his shoulders in defeat. He looked like a dog that had just gotten in trouble for peeing on the floor, its tail between its legs as it retreated to the corner. I didn't give in. Instead, I called my mom once the door closed behind him. My hands shook violently as I dialed her number.

"Can you talk?" I asked before explaining what just happened.

"Leave," my mom responded immediately. "Get out of there. Now." I had never heard her be so firm.

"Come home or go to a friend's house. Put as much distance between you two as you possibly can. What if he does something worse? You never know."

I took her advice and grabbed a small duffel bag. Without thinking, I threw in some clothes and essentials and left.

I'm coming over, I texted a friend from class who lived off-campus. *Can I spend the night?*

She didn't answer, but I knew I didn't even have to ask. She, her boyfriend, and their roommates left their door unlocked at all hours, letting people come and go as they pleased. No one would even know if I passed out on their couch.

Like clockwork, I forgave my boyfriend once he apologized. I was caught in his web, unable to free myself. The one thing I did, however, was remove my spare apartment key from his keychain in fear that he would seriously hurt me one day.

A few weeks later, I received an out-of-the-blue text from him in the early afternoon:

Hey babe, I'm waiting on your balcony. Naked. Hurry up and get home.

I was at my on-campus internship and dropped my phone on my desk as I read the notification.

He has to be drunk, I told myself. *How did he get into my apartment? What if this is it, the time he really hurts me?* I was officially scared.

I waited a few hours before heading home. As soon as I arrived—no boyfriend in sight, thankfully—I took my mom's more extreme advice. I packed what I could and headed home to my parents' house, desperate to put 145 miles between the two of us. I had already finished classes and was picking up extra shifts at my campus job, so nothing was tying me to San Luis Obispo.

Thankfully, I was leaving on my first trip, a generous graduation gift from my parents, in a few short days. During the two weeks I was gone, I traveled alone from Amsterdam through Brussels and London before meeting my mom and aunt in Scotland to explore the land where my dad was born. We ended the trip by spending a week in Paris, a city I had idolized since I was a teen.

During my Western European getaway, my sort-of ex and I kept in touch. Despite the fear I felt from our last two encounters, I craved his hugs and kisses, and it seemed both of us were willing to rekindle our three-year relationship. As soon as my mom, aunt, and I landed in San Francisco by way of Charles de Gaulle, I drove straight to his apartment in San Luis Obispo. I arrived late and severely jet-lagged, ready to fall into a deep slumber.

"I don't want you to sleep in my bed," he told me flatly. "You can sleep on the floor or the couch."

"Why not?" I asked, completely caught off guard. We often shared his twin bed, snuggling close to avoid rolling off.

"Just not feeling it." He shrugged.

My mind started reeling, thinking about everything I had done wrong. Within seconds, however, I stopped the thought spiral, too tired to think clearly. With the exhaustion hitting in full force, all I wanted to do was pass out.

"How about this?" I asked shortly. "I'll sleep on top of the sheet while you sleep under it. I really don't care. I just want to go to bed."

"Fine," he huffed. "Whatever."

I climbed into the bed, settling against the wall—under the comforter but on top of the sheet, as promised. I fell asleep as soon as my head hit the pillow.

In the morning, he wouldn't look me in the eye, didn't want to hug me, and definitely didn't want to kiss me. I didn't understand; I had just been away for two weeks, and the least he could do is give me a warm welcome home after telling me he missed me multiple times during the trip. Throughout the day, I pressed him to tell me what was going on until he eventually broke.

"I slept with someone else," he started.

Deep breaths, I coached myself.

"Who was she?" I asked, my voice shaking.

"It doesn't matter," he replied.

"It does," I shot back. "It matters to me."

Turns out, she was an acquaintance of mine—at one point, perhaps even a friend—who I had known since my freshman year. And even worse, she gave him chlamydia. No *wonder* he didn't want me sleeping in his bed. *What an asshole.*

I left in a frenzy, packing up my belongings and leaving for Carmel as quickly as possible, itching to get as far away from him as fast as I could.

4

FROM FAT TO FIT

Thankfully, I had a ten-day, all-expenses-paid trip to Israel to distract me from the swirling doubt, negativity, and anger going rampant in my mind.

I grew up Jewish, going to temple often three or four times per week for Hebrew school, Friday night services, Saturday or Sunday school, and Confirmation. During high school, I traveled to Los Angeles and New York with my Confirmation class to explore the Jewish culture in each city, but I couldn't wait to see the motherland and absorb a language, food, and religion that had been such an important part of my childhood.

Fortunately, I was able to do that through a program called Birthright Israel, a program for Jewish young adults between the ages of eighteen and thirty-two. They had hundreds of different programs to select from, and I chose one that was centered around the outdoors, hoping the added adventure would allow me to escape the immense and sudden heartbreak.

When I met my travel group at LAX, I felt eager yet unsure; I was by far the oldest on the trip—twenty-one—and felt out of place from the moment we stepped on the plane. For the majority of the fifteen-hour, thirty-eight-minute flight, my fellow travelers couldn't stop talking about how eager they were to legally consume alcohol every night, given Israel's lower drinking age of eighteen. Meanwhile, I was looking forward to the sights, sea, and shakshuka, totally uninterested in the getting drunk portion of our itinerary. Despite my unease, excitement and anticipation took over as we touched down at Ben Gurion airport.

Over the next ten days, we walked through the mystical city of Tzfat, which I instantly fell in love with, and enjoyed the laid-back feeling of Shabbat in the park. We floated in the Dead Sea, tasted our first bite of falafel, Israel's national dish, took a collective deep breath when we reached the top of Masada in the blazing afternoon sun, and danced with abandon in a Tel Aviv nightclub. We splashed through Hezekiah's underground water tunnels and went on a camel ride through the desert before enjoying a traditional Bedouin dinner while sitting on the floor of a large tent. I leaned my head against the Wailing Wall and murmured a prayer of gratitude for being able to participate in a tradition that had lasted centuries. The unforgettable trip did exactly what I hoped it would. It helped me escape our relationship and allowed me to be lost in a culture that I had been waiting my whole life to explore.

When I got home from Israel, I jumped straight into planning for my new life in San Jose. I secured an apartment, found a roommate on Craigslist, and moved everything from my apartment in San Luis Obispo to the Bay Area. It was a hectic few weeks, and it wasn't until I was settled into my new apartment that I took a moment to reflect on my Israel trip. I grabbed my laptop and settled onto my bed, my computer resting on my wide stomach. I brought up a Facebook album that held a random collection of photos that I mass-uploaded during the flight home. Scrolling through the thumbnails of beautiful scenery, I was mentally transported halfway across the world, recalling the feeling of awe I experienced as I stood on Israeli soil for the first time.

As soon as I enlarged the first photo of myself, I grimaced. The picture was from our first day in Jerusalem, when we visited the Haas Promenade, a thirteen-hundred-foot walkway that offered a panoramic view of the Old City. In the image, I was sitting in the center of a group of my newfound friends, smiling ear to ear under the sweltering Israeli sun. We were sitting on top of a wide cement bench, the city sprawled behind us like a postcard. Even with the stunning view, I couldn't focus on anything besides my legs. My thighs were taking up the entire photograph, save for my only slightly smaller belly, which was accentuated by the horizontal black and white stripes on my tank top. I couldn't help but compare myself to the girl sitting next to me, who looked glamorous in her white dress with her skinny body. I shivered, disgusted with myself, and flipped to the next photo. It wasn't much better.

The second photo was from a day later in the trip when we experienced the weightlessness of the Dead Sea for the first time. Rather than laughing about the dreadful moment when salt got stuck behind one of my contact lenses while I was half a mile out in the water, all I could do was think about how fake my smile looked. The girl who looked back at me from the photo stood in the water at calf level, wearing a bright blue tank top and a pair of black shorts with her white legs sticking out below her round belly. Her smile was forced, but her eyes told the real story. She was miserable. Looking at the photo, I wondered whether my body, not distance, had pushed my boyfriend to be with someone else.

I stood up, walked over to the full-length mirror hanging on my wall, and stripped down to my undergarments. I stared at myself, looking back at a chubby girl whose stomach was sticking out between her lime green sports bra and nude-colored underwear. I barely recognized myself, but I knew it was me behind the double chin, curved belly and touching thighs.

As I stared at my reflection set between the two gold lines of the mirror's frame, I searched for one thing that I liked about myself or my body.

Just one thing, I thought. *It can't be that hard.*

I started by looking at my hair, which was already starting to gray at twenty-one.

Thanks, Mom, I thought snarkily. Her hair turned gray at the same age, and she'd lovingly passed that gene down to me.

My gaze moved down my face, quickly noticing my brown eyes but getting sidetracked by my bushy eyebrows and big nose. The gap in between my top front teeth pushed me to look away, but I didn't—not yet.

As my eyes landed on my shoulders, I thought about how many people told me I was built for swimming: heavy, muscular, and big-boned, a euphemism for fat, which was confirmed when my eyes made their way down to my stomach.

My stomach was—and is—my least favorite part of my body. I haven't had a day, ever, that I can recall, when I haven't been embarrassed by my midsection. When I look in the mirror, even today, this is the part of me my eyes are drawn to first, often followed by thoughts of disgust then a spiral of denial.

Back in the room, in front of the gold mirror, I lingered on my stomach, recalling the numerous times people asked if I was pregnant.

As I glimpsed my thighs, I cringed. Sometimes, my legs were the one thing that I was proud of, knowing they gave me strength to walk, run, swim, and squat, but not this day. In that moment, they looked massive, exactly as they had in the photo.

I forced my eyes to look up and down my body multiple times, each time searching for just one thing I was proud of. Every time, my mind came up blank. I stood there for fifteen minutes tearing myself apart and coming to terms with the fact that everyone—my middle school bully, my boyfriend, friends, acquaintances—were right. I wasn't big-boned or muscular. I was fat.

When the realization hit, I slumped down to the floor and collapsed when I hit the soft carpet. I sprawled out on my back and stared up at the ceiling, completely giving up. I cursed myself for being fat. For letting my body get to that point. For not doing more to lose weight, get healthier, and get to a size six.

I saw that guilt and shame in that photo of the girl standing in front of the Dead Sea. To anyone else, I probably looked like a young girl who was enjoying the Mediterranean sun, but to me, I could only see the misery and grief that comes just weeks after a bad breakup, the disappointment that comes with giving up, and the shame of realizing you're not who you thought you were.

This guilt pushed me to commit to a diet for the first time ever. By that point, I had tried every diet under the sun but had given up when the going got tough. *Not this time*, I told myself. As I lay on the floor, I remembered a nutrition plan I bought two years prior for a whopping $150, which was a hell of a lot of money for a PDF that I never opened. I pulled myself over to the foot of the bed, close enough to grab my computer, and resumed my position of defeat. After hunting for a few minutes, I found the document and double-clicked to open it. It totaled 184 pages. *Let's do this.*

On the cover were two skinny, extremely fit women standing back to back in front of a very pink chevron background. They were wearing mix-and-match workout sets in hues of turquoise and peach, showing off their toned abs and muscular arms. With their wavy hair, they looked like they belonged on the beach year-round. In the first few pages, I read about the two trainers who designed the program and reviewed their checklist for success. On page nine, when they encouraged me to create a profile on Instagram to document their meals, workouts, and before-and-after photos, I didn't hesitate. I pulled out my phone, created a new Instagram account, and followed their instructions to take measurements, weigh in, and make a grocery list. I checked every box in their "getting started" list. By the time I read the first sixty-six pages discussing the plan and its guidelines, I felt the same way I always did at the start of a new challenge: inspired and ready to go all-in.

This is the moment, I told myself. *I'm going to change my life, literally overnight.*

I stood and confidently strode into the kitchen, ready to go through every single item as instructed. If an item was on their approved list, I kept it. If not, it went straight into the trash. An hour later, after going through the entire fridge, freezer, and pantry, I had zero groceries in the house. They were all in the dumpster.

In my excited state, I drove to the grocery store and bought every item on the program's grocery list: everything from pantry staples like pumpkin seeds and almond flour to cartoned egg whites, coconut yogurt, and a plant-based protein powder. I had already ordered a tub of the brand's protein powder online, but I needed something similar to hold me over until theirs arrived the following week. This was well before specialty health foods were available at neighborhood grocery stores, so I had to go to no less than four stores to buy all the groceries on their list. I spent hundreds of dollars on what was then a nonexistent salary (I was living off of a signing bonus I hadn't received yet), but at least my pantry, fridge, and freezer were stocked.

The next day, I meal prepped. The idea of cooking all thirty-five meals for the week in advance was new to me, but wanting to follow every rule to a T, I pulled out a pile of containers and got to work. I cooked for twelve hours straight, resulting in a stack of premade, pre-portioned meals that took up every inch of my half of the fridge and gave me a very sore back.

With the food handled, I started planning my exercise routine. They recommended two to three workouts a day:

a thirty-minute walk or high-intensity workout in the morning and a toning workout in the afternoon. If you were feeling up to it, you could add in a second thirty-minute cardio session with your afternoon workout or as a sunset stroll. Me being me, I did all three. Every day, seven days a week.

On top of this, the program encouraged me to meet up with other local members to bring the community offline and in person. I joined the San Francisco Bay Area Facebook group and attended, and even hosted, as many events as I could over the next few months. Throughout the summer, we met up for potlucks, cycling classes, outdoor workouts, hikes, or brunch almost every weekend. Before long, we became an integrated unit, bonding over our love of kale, green juice, and getting more and more likes on Instagram.

I genuinely loved this group of women. For the first time in my life, I felt like I had the friendships I had always craved—a group of uplifting and empowering women who supported each other instead of tearing each other apart or sabotaging their relationships. I connected with women of all ages and backgrounds, instantly finding common ground thanks to the program. Three of us even started training for a triathlon together, documenting our journey on a short-lived joint blog.

Every time I meal prepped, ate a meal, finished a workout, weighed in, or did anything related to the program, I snapped a photo and posted it to Instagram, dutifully listing the program-specific hashtags recommended in the PDF. In a short amount of time, my follower count grew from ten to one hundred to five hundred, and my goal shifted from weight loss to getting my before and after photo featured on the program's Instagram page.

For four months straight, I followed the strict eating and workout routine exactly as outlined. This was longer than any other program I'd committed to, and I only slipped up once or twice. I was eating well under twelve hundred calories a day and working out for hours on end, seven days a week. During triathlon training, I often did an eight-hundred-yard swim followed by an eight-mile bike ride, before finishing with a two-mile run. My off-days consisted of a two-or-three-mile walk or hike. While I'd love to say pushing myself this hard was for my health, I can't. It was for Instagram.

The more I worked out and the less I ate, the more weight I lost—and the more weight I lost, the more drastic my before and after photos became. What started as a simple meal plan spiraled into an unhealthy obsession with healthy eating, working out, and Instagram. I spent every waking hour on the app posting photos, connecting with other women in the community, and trying to grow my following.

When my follower count picked up, hitting one thousand, then two thousand, and then five thousand followers, I convinced myself I needed a solo blog, "because people were asking for it," even though no one was. I bought the domain laurenliveshealthy.com, changed my Instagram handle to "laurenliveshealthy" to match, and spent thousands upon thousands of dollars on a professionally -designed blog, courses to build my following, and products to feature on my site and social media—anything I could do to convince myself I was wanted by the internet.

Within a few months, my twenty-five-pound weight loss journey was featured on the program's newsletter and Instagram. I felt famous, like I was watching all of my dreams come true.

5

RACING FROM
COAST TO COAST

On October 6, 2013, I crossed the finish line of my first triathlon, a combination of swimming, biking, and running, and officially had the race bug. Scratch that; I had the dopamine bug.

Every time I posted a race-related photo on Instagram, whether it was an image of my training calendar hanging on my refrigerator door, a screenshot of my pre-race alarms the night before they went off—3:00 a.m., 3:15 a.m., and 3:30 a.m. with the accompanying text, "IT'S TIME," "Let's do this!" and "For real, let's GO," respectively—or a simple shot of an empty lap pool, my feed received more and more engagement. Because I started using hashtags beyond those of the health program, people from the online triathlon and training communities started following and commenting their support and encouragement. The likes and comments were a drug, an addiction I couldn't escape.

One weekend, I drove to San Francisco for a picnic on the beach with my new fitness friends. It was one of the city's rare beautiful sunny days, the always-present thick cloud of fog lifted so we could enjoy a deep dose of natural vitamin D. After filling our plates with the program-approved dishes that each of us brought, one of the ten or so girls in attendance proposed an idea.

"What do you think about signing up as a team for the Nike Women's Half Marathon next year?" She asked. "The San Francisco event happens every October, so we'd have plenty of time to train."

At the time, the Nike Women's Half Marathon was the pinnacle of road races, considered to be the largest women's race in the world. There were two events, one in Washington, DC, in April and another in San Francisco in October, that brought together tens of thousands of women to support the Leukemia and Lymphoma Society, an organization dedicated to finding cures for blood cancers and ensuring patients have access to treatment.

Another girl pulled out her phone to look up the details. "Looks like it's a lottery system," she explained while continuing to scroll. "It appears teams have a better chance at getting accepted than individuals."

"Let's do it," a third girl said. "We can sign up as a group."

"I'm in," a fourth added.

"Me too," chimed a fifth girl.

I had never in my life considered running a half marathon. The longest I had run was during the sprint triathlon, which was 3.1 miles. I barely survived; there was *no way* I could run ten miles on *top* of that. No way in hell.

All eyes turned my way, waiting to see if I'd participate or not. Although I despised running, I hated the idea of feeling left out even more. After a few seconds, I begrudgingly muttered, "I'm in, too." We all laughed at my hesitation before the conversation quickly turned to setting personal records.

"I want to run sub-two hours," one of the girls announced. I pulled out my phone to calculate what that would mean: nine minutes and nine seconds per mile. My eyes widened at the screen. If I was lucky, I could maintain a thirteen-minute pace—and that's if I was running the whole time. It would be a miracle if I crossed the finish line in under three hours. I instantly regretted saying yes, knowing I'd be the slowest of the pack.

It's not about the time, I told myself over and over again. *It's about crossing the finish line and supporting a good cause.*

After losing my aunt to cancer during my senior year of high school, I became passionate about volunteering for St. Jude Children's Research Hospital, a leading children's hospital that specialized in treating childhood cancer. This would be the perfect opportunity to continue raising awareness for cancer research while pushing my body to its physical limit. Plus, I'd get some amazing content for my blog and Instagram. Adding #WeRunSF, the hashtag runners were encouraged to use leading up to and during the race, to my photos would put my content in front of an audience of millions.

When I got home, I googled "half marathon training plan" and instantly felt overwhelmed yet encouraged. *I can do this,* I told myself over and over again. I downloaded a free plan, wrote the details of each workout on my calendar, and committed to not only finishing but running the entire race. This was happening. I was going to be a half marathoner.

The next morning was like any other. I woke up early to make a program-approved breakfast. As I was walking from the kitchen to the patio, preparing to enjoy my meal in the early morning sunshine, I stopped in my tracks. I stood mid-step in the middle of my living room, my left hand balancing a plate with protein waffle drizzled with maple syrup, and my right holding a collagen latte in my favorite llama mug.

Why not try for both races? I asked myself.

The Nike Women's Half Marathon was a lottery system, meaning it was pure luck whether you got accepted or not. From what my friends said, we had a better chance of getting in if we applied as a team, which I had already committed to for the San Francisco race. I figured putting my name in the hat for the DC event couldn't hurt. If I got in, I would be one of few who did coast-to-coast races. If I didn't get in, nothing would change. I had to try.

The night before the DC application opened, I set an alarm to go off two minutes before the submission page went live. When my alarm blared, I stopped everything and logged on to the registration website, hitting refresh every two seconds until, finally, after what felt like a million clicks, it let me submit my contact information, t-shirt size, and estimated pace. Once the confirmation page appeared, I crossed my fingers, toes, and eyes that I would get accepted. The more I thought about it, the more convinced I was that I *needed* to do the DC race.

Despite knowing the results of the lottery wouldn't be announced for weeks, I checked my email every ten minutes to see if there were any updates. I was *desperate* to participate in both events, eager to get a professional race photo for my feed and a famed Tiffany's finisher's necklace at the end of each. In January 2014, I received the first email I had been waiting for.

Your Entry to the 2014 Nike Women's Half Marathon DC has been Accepted, the subject line read. My breath hitched as I opened the email, seeing the text, "On April 27, 2014, you will join fifteen thousand women as you conquer the Nike Women's Half Marathon in Washington, DC." Below that was my five-digit bib number. I was *in*. This was really happening.

"We're going to DC!" I yelled to Matt, my boyfriend of just three months.

We'd met in August the prior year, connecting over our jobs in marketing. Despite a tumultuous first date—I showed up forty-five minutes late—and an awkward ending to our second date, we'd found our rhythm and officially started dating in October.

In fact, he met my parents at my first race, a triathlon in Santa Cruz, California, soon after we met. I extended him a courtesy invite to watch the race, not at all expecting him to show up. His close friend was visiting from out of state, and they had gone out the night before. I figured they'd want to spend the morning sleeping in after a late night out; plus, we had only been together a few weeks by this point. When I crossed the finish line, I was shocked to see him standing at the finish line with two of his friends who had quickly become my friends, too.

I ran over to give him a sweaty hug, said hello to our friends, and waved over my parents, who were standing just a few feet away. I made introductions before turning back to him to ask where his friend from out of town was.

"He didn't want to wake up early, so I left him at home," Matt replied. "It was important for me to be at the finish line cheering you on." He gave me a quick kiss, not caring that our friends or my parents were watching.

My bottom lip started to quiver while I held back tears. It was such a different experience than I'd had with my ex-boyfriend. I constantly questioned whether he was ashamed or embarrassed of me; by contrast, I had no doubt this man wanted to be with me. I stepped back to catch my breath, letting my parents, Matt, and our two friends engage in small talk. Matt wouldn't let me go far, though; he grabbed my hand and squeezed, letting me know he was right there.

After I gathered my gear, the four of us—me, Matt, and our two friends—said goodbye to my parents to meet the girls I competed with for a celebratory breakfast. On the walk to the restaurant, Matt grabbed my hand, showing the world that I was his, even though we weren't officially together. Unbeknownst to us, one of our friends snapped a photo of us from behind. To this day, it's one of my favorite pictures. Matt and I are walking together, me on his right side. I'm wearing a black-and-white leopard dress, my muscular thighs sticking out above my nude suede flats, while he's in his classic uniform of jeans and a gray t-shirt. His short, light brown hair grazes the top of the photo. My left hand is intertwined with his right, and we're lost in conversation. It's a candid moment of pure, authentic love—before we knew that was what it was.

After breakfast, everyone said their goodbyes, and Matt and I headed our separate ways. The hour-long drive back to my house took me on a windy, mountainous highway known for fatal car accidents. When I merged on the highway, I glanced in the rear-view mirror, and, to my surprise, saw Matt's face in the car behind me. Not only did he wait for me to pull out of the participant parking, he followed me the full hour to my house, just to make sure I didn't fall asleep at the wheel in my post-race exhaustion. My parents and I all fell in love with him that day.

I immediately became obsessed with racing, signing up for one event per month on average. Although he preferred to sleep in until 10:00 a.m. on weekends, Matt woke up at three or four in the morning on the days I had a race so he could make me a pre-race peanut butter and jelly sandwich, drive me to the start line, and wait for me at the finish line. He documented each race on his cell phone, snapping dozens of images to look back on and weed through after.

For my birthday, my parents gave me a DSLR, something I was eager to use for food photography to improve the quality of photos on my blog. What I didn't realize was that Matt was excited to use it, too.

"Is there an easy way to take pictures?" he asked the first time I asked him to hold the camera.

After I got the camera, I took a food photography workshop where I learned to set the aperture, ISO, and shutter speed myself in manual mode. Matt was used to watching me adjust the camera settings before, during, and after each shot, but he wasn't as familiar with how the camera and its settings worked.

"You can put it on 'creative auto' and the camera will do the work for you," I said before showing him how to change it to the setting I was referring to. "Then you can look into the viewfinder and click the shutter button. You can look at the screen after to see if you like the photo."

At each event thereafter, Matt became my personal race photographer. He would try to catch me from a couple points during the race and started to get creative with which angle he took photos from. Although he didn't participate in the races as an athlete, this was his way of playing a part in each one.

We had never traveled together, but I knew I couldn't do the DC half marathon without him waiting at the finish line. On Friday, April 25, just three days after moving in together, we boarded a cross-country flight from San Jose, California, to Washington, DC. We landed well after dark and, after checking into our hotel, walked into the first restaurant we saw. When we asked the hostess for a table for two, we got a strange look, but they responded, "We have one table open. Follow me this way." As soon as we walked into the dining room, we looked at each other with wide eyes. Every single person in the restaurant was dressed to the nines in black tie apparel; we were in jeans and leggings, straight off the plane. Minutes after we sat down, Matt spilled his water all over the table, bringing even more attention to our out-of-place presence. It's safe to say our trip wasn't off to the best start.

The next day, we made our way to the expo center to pick up my bib, t-shirt, and other gear for the following day's race. As soon as I stepped into the race village, my excitement flew off the charts, the energy radiating off the other participants and various tents. After picking up my runner's packet, I asked Matt if we could stop by the merchandise tent. When we turned the corner, we saw the line was easily two hundred and fifty people deep. I felt bad, but I really wanted a sweatshirt to commemorate the event.

"Do you mind waiting?" I asked while bouncing on my toes like an eager child.

I looked over at Matt with big puppy dog eyes, hoping that would help convince him to stay, but he started talking before he caught my eye.

"Absolutely," he said without hesitation. "We can do anything you want. This is your weekend."

Over forty-five minutes later, I stepped up to the table and bought a thin, over-priced bright red running sweater with the event logo on the front chest. After paying and making our way through the sea of people, we stopped at a street corner so I could put on the sweatshirt. I dropped my bag on the sidewalk and slipped it on over my tank top. I didn't take it off until the next morning—not until I walked up to the start line, handing it to Matt to hold while I ran.

The 13.1 miles through Washington, DC, were stunning; I ran through rows of cherry blossom-lined streets as I made my way past national landmarks. The race started in front of the National Archives before running past the US Capitol building, the National Gallery, the Smithsonian Museum of Natural History, the Jefferson Memorial, the World War II Memorial, the Lincoln Memorial, and other landmarks before circling back around to finish the same place it started. I had never been to DC before, and touring the city in this way was truly unique.

Throughout the course, a few photographers were snapping photos, and I was acutely aware of each one, *especially* the photographer at the finish line. From the moment I entered my name in the lottery, I had a vision of what my final photo would look like: my hands raised in victory, pointing to the sky, smiling straight into the camera. When I saw the finish line and the photographers, I did just that. Despite the intense cramp in my left calf, I put on a smile, raised my hands in triumph, and pointed upward.

At two hours, fifty-nine minutes, and forty-nine seconds, I crossed the finish line. *I did it.* I finished my first half marathon in under three hours—and got the dream photo I hoped for.

Upon crossing the finish line, I walked through the throngs of participants, making sure to collect a Tiffany's finishers necklace from a firefighter in a tuxedo, a unique aspect of the Nike Women's Half Marathon series. After a few minutes, I spotted Matt in the crowd, waiting patiently with my camera hanging around his neck.

"You did it!" he exclaimed. He always seemed prouder of me than I was of myself.

"I can't believe it," I told him, panting. "My legs feel like they're going to collapse any second."

"Want to go back to the hotel to rest?" he asked, already starting to walk in that direction.

"Yes, please," I said, limping behind him. "We can explore DC as regular tourists tomorrow."

Two days later, we arrived back home in the Bay Area. Every nook and cranny of my body was sore and inflamed from running 13.1 miles, walking eight miles the next day, and then sitting six hours on a plane. It hurt to sit, stand, lie down, walk, and go to the bathroom. I was miserable.

To distract myself, I refreshed my email every few minutes, eagerly waiting for the professional photos to arrive. Eventually, I received a notification on my phone that they were available, so I rushed to click the link. Instead of individualized photos, we got access to a large folder and had to look for ourselves, identified by our bib number. I spent what felt like hours scrolling through the thousands of photos from the finish line until I found the one I was looking for: my bright blue shirt, bib pinned to the front, with my arms pointing to the sky. The capitol building was perfectly centered in the background, a symbolic reminder of where I started and ended the race. The photo was even better than I envisioned.

A laugh escaped my mouth when I peered closer. Peeking out from behind my left shoulder was an older woman with the same exact stance: hands raised, pointer fingers facing the sky in victory. Despite our immense age gap, we looked like twins. I immediately posted the photo to Instagram.

"#IRanDC" I wrote in the caption. Over the next twenty-four hours, it got more likes than any other photo on my feed.

6

ESCAPING ALCATRAZ

Almost every swimmer has one item on their bucket list: "escaping" Alcatraz.

I grew up visiting San Francisco on a monthly basis, so I was very familiar with the jailhouse island that sat in the middle of the San Francisco Bay. Given the distance from shore, cold water temperature, and strong currents, "The Rock," as many called it, was designed to be escape-proof. According to the FBI, only fourteen escape attempts were made during the prison's twenty-nine-year tenure, and nearly all of the thirty-six inmates who attempted were caught or didn't survive. Only three men, who escaped together on June 11, 1962, may have made it out alive. The FBI and other government agencies were unable to determine whether they survived or not and closed the case after seventeen years without answers.

I never really considered doing the swim until I received an email promoting an event called the Alcatraz Challenge. According to the email, participants swim 1.5 miles from the historic island to San Francisco's mainland before running seven miles out and back across the Golden Gate Bridge. Because I had just finished the half marathon in Washington, DC, I was in the best shape of my life, confident I could do both the swim and the run with little training. I signed up on a whim one month before the event and only did one formal training session.

Swimmers couldn't participate in the event if they didn't sign into one of the briefings, so Matt and I drove up to San Francisco the day before the swim to ensure I could attend. On the way to Fort Mason, where the meeting would be held, I snapped a photo of Alcatraz on my phone and posted it to Instagram.

Oh hey, Alcatraz, I wrote in the caption. *See you bright and early tomorrow.*

Matt dropped me off for the safety briefing a few minutes early so I could settle into a chair toward the back of the small seating area. At 5:00 p.m. on the dot, an older gentleman walked up to a projector reminiscent of my high school statistics class and told us he had swum Alcatraz every Wednesday evening for years on end.

"I'm essentially an expert at escaping the island," he said, receiving a laugh and half-hearted cheers from the crowd.

I saw an aerial photo of Alcatraz and the San Francisco shoreline, where we would be swimming to, flash up on the screen behind him.

"This is the important part," he said seriously.

"The current is so strong that it can pull you out to sea if you miss one particular point. Your line of sight needs to change multiple times throughout the swim to make sure you land at Crissy Beach. If you forget to swim toward just one of these landmarks, you'll fall completely off course," he continued, pointing at a map with no less than six landmarks circled.

AKA, you're screwed, I narrated in my head.

If he was saying this with such certainty, I knew it was serious. My goal for the night went from eating as much pasta as humanly possible—a practice athletes called "carb-loading" where you eat a massive amount of carbs the night before a race to fuel your body for the following day—to memorizing the order of landmarks that I would have to look for during the swim.

"Don't worry," he continued. "We'll be able to see you and will pick you up if you're falling off course. We have kayakers, boats, first aid responders, and the Coast Guard lining your swim so you won't get lost."

He quickly added, "You might not be able to see us, but, I promise, we will always be able to see you." I was officially freaked out.

The next morning, Matt, my dog, Gigi, and I arrived to the race site at 4:00 a.m. so I could lay out my running gear in the participant corral. I pulled on my triathlon suit, a tank top and matching shorts designed to go from swimming to running without changing. After setting up my station, I nibbled at my standard Matt-made peanut butter and jelly sandwich, which was carefully wrapped in a paper towel and stored inside a plastic bag. My stomach was woozy from nerves, and it took me a good fifteen minutes to finish the sandwich; usually it only took two. When I was done eating, I pulled on my jet-black wetsuit to keep me warm in the chilly water. I overheard other swimmers saying the water was expected to be around sixty degrees Fahrenheit, a far cry from the eighty-degree pools I was accustomed to swimming in.

After giving Matt a big hug, I made my way to the shuttle, which took us down to the beach for a mandatory orientation. At 8:00 a.m. sharp, I walked onto the ferry along with the other participants and stepped into a big open room. I took a seat on the floor, unable to stand on my shaky legs. Before the boat started moving, I zipped up my wetsuit, eager to start getting in the race mindset.

"Unzip your wetsuit!" someone yelled at me a few minutes later. "Someone died last year because they zipped up their wetsuit on the ferry ride over."

Terrified, I scrambled to find the zipper pull hanging behind my back so I could free myself. The man went on to explain that the shock of the cold water on the person's body caused their heart rate and blood pressure to skyrocket, leading to a fatal heart attack in the water.

"Zip it up when you get in line to jump and you'll be good," he advised.

I turned away, needing to home in on my breathing in an effort to calm my rampant mind.

What the hell was I thinking? I'm not ready. I'm going to die out there. Oh my god, I can't remember the order of the viewpoints. What if I forget and get dragged out to sea? I really need to use the bathroom; I should have tried to go before we got on the boat. What's going on? Oh no. Why is the boat making a circle? Does that mean we're almost there? Oh my god, people are lining up, getting ready to jump in. Someone's zipping up their wetsuit. It's time. Crap. Is it too late to back out? I should have trained more. I'm not ready. Can I just stay on the boat? Oh my god, oh my god, oh my god.

I took a deep breath and pulled my hair back into a bun before pulling on my first cap, followed by my goggles. Over my goggles, I pulled on the bright green cap they required us to wear.

"It's time," someone said over the speaker a few minutes later. "Line up by the back of the boat and jump in. When you hit the water, remember to get out of the way of the other swimmers jumping in behind you. Good luck."

When I got to the front of the line, I closed my eyes and leapt off the edge of the boat. As soon as I hit the water, I sputtered, spitting out salt water as my head surfaced above the choppy waves. I took a few strokes so I wouldn't get hit by the onslaught of swimmers behind me and, as soon as I was in a safe zone, I completely froze.

For what felt like five minutes, I treaded water trying to get my bearings. I was just a few feet away from where I had jumped in the water and was able to float easily thanks to my wetsuit. I was shivering, freezing in the chilly water. I was so cold that I went to the bathroom, in hopes that the urine would warm me up, even just one degree. I was desperate.

After acclimating to the water temperature and spotting my first landmark to swim toward, I took off. I did what they told us to do in the safety briefings: take a few strokes and look up to make sure you're swimming in the right direction. With each stroke, a wave would push me up and pull me back down so forcefully that water would splash over my head, into my mouth, and into my goggles. I couldn't swim like I did in the pool with my head down and clean freestyle strokes; I had to constantly keep my neck tilted up, which ended up pulling my hips down further into the water, causing me to go even slower and repeat the process of swallowing water. I had never swum so hard in my life.

"You're one of few people who will ever get a 360-degree view of San Francisco, Oakland, the Golden Gate Bridge, the Bay Bridge, and Alcatraz from the water," the presenter had said during the safety briefing. "At one point during the swim, make sure to take a moment to look up and soak in the views."

Halfway through the swim, I took his advice. Expecting to feel awe and joy at the unparalleled views, I was absolutely terrified. No matter which direction I turned, I couldn't see anyone—not another swimmer, not a kayaker, not one of the first aid boats. I was completely and utterly alone; just me, massive waves, and the great white shark that was spotted a couple of weeks before. *Great.* I put my head down and swam even harder.

When I finally made it to shore, I crawled onto the sand, feeling like I literally just escaped Alcatraz. I had never pushed my body so hard in my life, and now I had to run seven miles. *What the hell was I thinking?* I asked myself over and over again as I made my way to the corral to put on my running shoes. I couldn't find Matt, Gigi, my parents, or my aunt in the crowd as I ran past, but I assumed they were there cheering, feeling as relieved as I was to be out of the water. Within a few short minutes, I was off and running.

I started out at a good pace until I came upon what looked like the steepest hill I had ever seen in my life. After trudging up, I tackled a few sets of stairs to get to the top of the Golden Gate Bridge before winding my way through groups of tourists to get to the north side of the bridge. Each time I passed someone with a bib on, we'd smile and hype each other up.

"Almost there," they'd tell me. "Just a little further until you can turn around."

"You've got this," I'd reply. "See you at the finish line!"

When I reached the turnaround on the other side of the bridge, I started bawling. Looking out over the Bay and seeing how far I still had to run—back across the whole bridge and down a good part of the marina—seemed unfathomable. Every muscle in my body was hurting, and every joint aching. I sobbed in discomfort as I limped back across the bridge. Halfway across, I stopped to look at the view.

You just did that, I congratulated myself, looking out at the water and seeing how far Alcatraz was from the mainland. *You swam from Alcatraz and now you're running across the iconic Golden Gate Bridge. It doesn't matter if you come in last; all that matters is that you make it back.*

I put one foot in front of the other, determined to jog the rest of the way across the bridge. I cursed the stairs when I came across them—going down in pain and severe exhaustion was exponentially harder than going up—and let out a huge breath of relief when I arrived at the straight shot of pavement in the Presidio. I just had a little longer to go.

My entire body was cramping. My left knee was absolutely *killing* me, and my right ankle felt like it had taken a beating. I had blisters on both feet, and I was more exhausted than I had ever been before. When the finish line came into view, I broke down in tears again.

"Look! It's Gigi's mom!" I heard over the loudspeaker as I crossed the finish line, a smile crossing my face and a laugh escaping my lips. Even at my biggest moment, Gigi was the star of the show.

Matt, my parents, and my aunt walked over to congratulate me, but I pushed right past them, looking for somewhere, anywhere, I could sit down. Between the pain, the thank-God-it's-over relief, and the shock and awe that I actually crossed the finish line, I was crying harder than I ever had in my life. Once I collapsed onto the side of a planter, Matt kneeled at my side and put his hand on my shoulder.

"What do you need?" he asked. I couldn't respond through the tears. At my silence, he pulled me in for a hug.

"I'm so proud of you," he whispered into my ear.

"Thanks," I responded back. "I'm proud of me too."

7

THE NEVER-ENDING CLEANSE

Growing up, my family often joked that my mom was the worst cook in America. She could only make three dishes: orzo with butter, Ritz crackers with peanut butter and jelly, and for some reason, lamb chops, which my brother and I called "shamlocks." Other than that, we were doomed if she stepped into the kitchen, destined to eat something wildly overcooked or completely raw. There was no in between.

Because of my mom's lack of cooking skills and my parents' busy schedules, we often ate out. We alternated between all of our go-tos: a family-owned taqueria, where I'd order a cheesy quesadilla; a local pizzeria, my go-to pie topped with sausage, mushrooms, and black olives; a sit-down restaurant, where I'd order tortellini with butter, nothing else; and a burger joint, where I'd get a plain burger, nothing on it, with a basket of fries. Unless they were on pizza, I very rarely ate veggies, and salads were definitely out of the question unless they were doused in ranch.

When we ate at home, it was most likely a mix-and-match selection from the hot food bar at our local supermarket. When I went out with friends, we primarily did drive-through. Jack in the Box was a favorite; their crispy mozzarella sticks were one of my go-to after-school treats. From Taco Bell, I'd order a Crunch Wrap Supreme. Chicken McNuggets and fries dipped in sweet-and-sour and honey barbecue sauce from McDonald's was also a regular occurrence. If my friends and I wanted a nicer meal, we went to Chipotle.

Even when I was alone, I defaulted to food as a source of comfort. On more than one occasion, I went to my favorite seafood restaurant and ordered a clam chowder bread bowl with a side of curly fries. I ate every last crumb, leaving no trace behind. On the way home, I stopped at a drive-through to order a medium vanilla milkshake, making sure to finish it by the time I arrived home so I could throw it in the trash bin outside without anyone noticing. By the time I'd walk in the door, it was 6:00 p.m. "What's for dinner?" I'd ask my parents. I sought comfort in the extra calories, but they only left me feeling emptier than before.

When I wasn't indulging, I was trying the latest fad diet. During my Weight Watchers phase in high school, my mom would drive me to the mall every Monday afternoon so we could do our weekly weigh-in and participate in the day's discussion. I tried to cheat the system by starving myself throughout the week and drinking a liter of water before walking into the building. It worked; I often lost multiple pounds a week, a cause for celebration.

At one meeting, an older woman sat down next to me as we were waiting for the presentation to start.

"You don't look like you need to be here," she told me. At 5'10" and one hundred eighty pounds, I believed the opposite.

No matter which diet I tried—Weight Watchers, SlimFast, the South Beach Diet, Atkins—it lasted for a couple weeks before I caved and indulged in pizza, pasta, a burger, or a combination of them all because I was *starving*. The cycle continued through college, even getting to a point of desperation where I tried weight loss pills.

"You look *amazing*," one of my sorority sisters commented one afternoon when I showed up to the house for an event. "What have you been doing?"

"Just eating healthy and working out," I shrugged. I couldn't bring myself to admit I had been taking laxatives that I found on the sale shelves of the drug store.

In 2013, when I overhauled my diet as part of the women's health program, I went all-in. Their nutrition plan came with a strict meal-by-meal guide and hundreds of recipes, marked with which meal they were "approved" for.

The first meal of the day was to be eaten within ninety minutes of waking up and was centered around protein. My go-to breakfast was Greek yogurt topped with strawberries, banana, and carob chips to make a healthy take on a banana split. Along with breakfast, I chugged an apple cider vinegar drink to boost my metabolism and get my system going. My mid-morning snack, essentially a second breakfast, was often a protein smoothie, fresh green juice, or a piece of fruit. More often than not, lunch was a salad with a drizzle of oil and a squeeze of lemon as dressing. Because I was eating salads so often, I forced myself to learn to tolerate them.

The afternoon was the hardest part. The program encouraged me to avoid dairy and limit starches after lunch, including classics like bread, pasta, and potatoes, but also corn, squash, and sweet potatoes, among other foods. Instead, I was encouraged to enjoy protein and healthy fat-based meals like hummus and veggies, a protein smoothie, or a plain avocado. The same rules applied for dinner. I often made a stir-fry with beans or tofu to get me through my last meal. If I absolutely needed dessert, I had Greek yogurt sprinkled with cinnamon. While it sounds like a full day of meals, the portions were minuscule in comparison to what I was used to eating. I was diligent about tracking—everything from weight to measurements—and found I often ate well below the recommended minimum of twelve hundred calories.

The first holiday season on this diet was rough. In addition to following the nutrition guidelines, I committed to eating a vegetarian diet, much to the dismay of my family. Our Thanksgiving meals were typically served buffet-style with all the traditional dishes: turkey, honey-baked ham, mashed potatoes and gravy, stuffing, fluffy dinner rolls, and, of course, dessert. Our Hanukkah table housed challah, matzo ball soup, crispy latkes with applesauce and sour cream, slow-cooked brisket, and my all-time favorite: kugel, a sweet Jewish pasta dish. On Christmas, we went out for Chinese food, where I always had a cup of wonton soup followed by a plate of sweet and sour chicken, broccoli beef, and fried rice. Food has always been the way to my heart, but I was at a point in my weight loss journey where I wouldn't break the rules. I never cheated, even though I was seriously tempted.

"Don't worry about me," I told my parents before one of these meals. "I'll bring and eat a salad." They knew as well as I did that I would rather starve than eat a plate of vegetables on Thanksgiving.

My dad, the chef of the family, showed up to my aunt's house with a vegetarian main dish that met most of my needs.

"It's acorn squash stuffed with wild rice," he told me proudly.

"Thanks, Dad," I replied, even though the thought of squash paled in comparison to the golden-brown brined turkey sitting on the counter. My mouth watered each time I glanced over at it.

I made it through the holiday season as a vegetarian, just in time to start a cleanse for the New Year. I followed a popular food blogger who released a five-day vegan cleanse and thought that would be the perfect opportunity to take my diet to the next level. I purchased the twenty-five-dollar plan and walked straight into Matt's office to see if he would do it with me.

"How long is it?" he asked hesitantly.

"Just five days," I replied. "Totally doable; five meals a day."

I quickly added, "It promises we won't be hungry."

Cleanses weren't his thing, but supporting my goals was.

"I'll do all the cooking and prep," I promised. "All you have to do is eat."

"I guess..." he said unenthusiastically, his voice trailing off at the end. "If it'll help you."

I had never seen him eat a vegan meal before unless I had cooked it for us. Cheese was by far his favorite food, so his agreeing to join was a big deal.

I printed out the grocery list and headed to the store, filling my cart with more vegetables than I had ever seen in my life, even compared to when I strictly followed the women's nutrition plan. When I got home, I unpacked four large grocery bags and started meal prepping for the next five days. The plan called for one smoothie, two juices, one salad, and one soup or roasted veggie meal per day, each a completely different recipe, all made from scratch.

The first two days weren't bad; despite our stomachs growling nonstop, we were both able to push through. Things went downhill on day three. Lunch was supposed to be a butternut squash soup with nutmeg. The recipe called for two tablespoons of nutmeg, far more than the sprinkle or quarter of a teaspoon I had ever used in a recipe before. Wanting to follow the cleanse exactly as stated, I measured out two full tablespoons of ground nutmeg, crinkling my nose as I added it to the blender. In an instant, our small kitchen smelled like pumpkin pie, minus the pumpkin and cinnamon.

We each went to work armed with a bowl of soup to enjoy over lunch. When I sat down in the cafeteria to enjoy mine, I took a bite and promptly spat it out. I couldn't taste anything besides nutmeg. It was the worst spoonful of soup—or any food, for that matter—that I had ever tasted in my life. I put the lid back on the container, unable to eat anymore, opting to skip lunch even though I was starving.

When Matt got home that night, he unpacked the myriad of containers I sent with him to work. I was surprised to see that he ate half of the soup.

"How did you eat that?" I asked in awe. "I couldn't eat more than a bite. It was disgusting."

"I didn't want you to think I didn't like your food, so I powered through until I couldn't anymore," he said with a slight grimace. "Plus, I was starving. But I have to tell you. It was the worst soup I've ever had."

We burst out laughing. When in doubt, we were always on the same page.

This cleanse set off a chain of food challenges. During the month of February, I ate a completely vegan, plant-based diet, which seemed to be the latest trend according to the food bloggers I followed. In March, as a way to "reset" my diet, I followed a strict five-day cleanse by the creators of the women's health program. Unsurprisingly, I lost a good chunk of weight within the five days, given the program was even more restrictive than their everyday guidelines.

The following month, I tried Whole30, a popular elimination diet that promised to nix cravings, improve sleep and energy, and reduce anxiety, chronic pain, digestive issues, and skin conditions—all while losing weight healthfully and sustainably. For thirty days, I followed the strict clean-eating plan, eating the same roasted vegetable bowl topped with a runny egg for nearly every meal because I wasn't sure what else I could eat. I lost over ten pounds but realized I love food too much to follow such a strict plan and resorted back to the standard American diet soon after my thirty days ended, allowing myself to indulge in pizza for the first time in what felt like years. Having a full belly for the first time in months, I felt like me again, but extreme guilt pushed through, and I cursed myself for falling off the bandwagon.

To get myself back on track, I resorted to a seven-day cleanse, also by the founders of the women's health program. The difference between this program and their five-day one was the lack of carbs, not even fruit. Each day, I ate about eight hundred calories, all while training for a half marathon and a long-distance triathlon. By the end of the week, I had lost five more pounds and had the before-and-after pictures—and a comment from one of the program founders on my Instagram post—to prove it.

"Amazing!!!!" she wrote.

What she and those who followed my journey on Instagram and the blog didn't see was how weak I was. I couldn't get out of bed. When I tried to get up on the morning after the cleanse, I collapsed, just barely catching myself on the edge of the bed before hitting the ground. Despite my weak knees and dark bags under my eyes, I felt proud. I was the thinnest I had ever been in my adult life, and I was receiving more support than ever before. Watching the amount of likes on my before-and-after photo reach fifty, and then one hundred, and then two hundred was well worth a little discomfort.

8

HELLO, HATERS

About a year into blogging, I made the mistake of googling myself.

In that time, I worked feverishly to optimize my site for search engines and wanted to see what came up when I searched my blog name. I typed "Lauren lives healthy" into the search bar and, as expected, saw the link to my homepage. Out of curiosity, I skimmed down the first page of search results to see what other content came up. Halfway down the page, a link caught my eye:

Fitness IGers | Page 86 | Instagram | Forums, the heading read.

Next to the publish date, August 14, 2015, the snippet read, "anyone follow laurenliveshealthy? she sort of irks me but i cant pinpoint why."

My stomach dropped.

I looked to the next search result, also from the same site but with a different snippet: "http://www. laurenliveshealthy.com is my new fluff reversperation/ hate read. Overall she's fairly harmless, just kind of dumb (maple syrup is ...""

I couldn't *not* click. I needed to know how that sentence ended.

The link led me to a forum about the health program, tearing the two founders and their followers, including me, apart. Hundreds of pages had people going back and forth, talking shit about people in the community. As I read through the page, I found the post mentioned in the search result:

> *[Lauren Lives Healthy] is my new fluff reversperation/ hate read. Overall she's fairly harmless, just kind of dumb (maple syrup is healthy! cookies are healthy if they don't have flour, just ignore the huge glob of almond butter, the coconut sugar, and the chocolate chips!). She's a [program] "member" and goes on regularly about how great the program is. Seems to think "research" is the same thing as "reading a company's promotional materials." Gives off a definite vibe of self-importance and is decidedly guilty of overindulging in the word "indulge."*

The post went on for five lengthy paragraphs. One section, in particular, caught me completely off guard:

> *Last, she sure doesn't seem to have problems with tossing money at health/fitness/weight loss stuff... She does seem to have an actual full-time job, I'll give her that, though her spending seems to be a bit on the high side relative to what I'd guess her salary is and the [cost of living] in her area.*

> *So of course, as with many [healthy living bloggers], I'm wondering if there's family money or if she's just going to be incredibly broke in another five to ten years*

when she tries to add things like a mortgage or family to her life.

As I read, my breath caught, my heart raced, and my jaw hurt from clenching too tightly. I simultaneously felt broken and betrayed while telling myself, "They can't see into my bank account! How do they know how much I have in savings or whether I even want a house or a family? I don't even know those things."

I instantly felt nauseated, even more so as I scrolled down the page. A handful of follow-up comments agreed with this initial post, slicing even deeper into my open wound. Some provided constructive feedback—too many affiliate links, for example, which I took to heart—but I couldn't process the rest of it. The piece about my salary and future, in particular, stuck with me. At twenty-three years old, *I* didn't even know what my future held.

Furthermore, the person who posted that comment seemed to have followed me since the beginning. They quoted my weight loss journey in depth, noting the exact amount of weight I gained, then lost, then gained, then lost, over the last year. It was incredibly in depth for a hate comment, and I imagined they spent a good ten to fifteen minutes, at least, writing it out. I couldn't fathom how people made that much time in their day to follow someone and then write about them if they didn't like the person. There was an unfollow button for a reason.

Trying to make light of the situation, I took a screenshot and sent it to Matt, my mom, and a couple close friends to gain sympathy. I assured them I'd be fine, even though I knew I wouldn't. I also took to Instagram, writing a post about how hurtful it was to read those comments and to see people who I had never met say such personal things that they couldn't possibly have insight into. I was never good at letting go of negativity if I saw myself as the victim.

It didn't work.

I got sucked into the site, trying to figure out what it was and why it existed. At the top of the about page, I read that it was created in 2008 as the internet's first blogger/influencer-focused gossip site. The forums were created two years later so users could discuss people who hadn't been featured on the homepage.

I was in awe that such a terrible place existed online. I tried to keep going as if nothing happened, but I couldn't. Guilt, shame, and numbness washed over me as I crumbled inside. I wasn't mad at the trolls; I was sad, hurt, and disappointed in myself. I believed it was *my* fault that I was featured on the forum; if I were skinnier, healthier, and a better blogger, they wouldn't have anything awful to say about me. With that in mind, I kept starving myself, trying to become the person I thought they wanted me to be.

As the months went on, hate comments continued to pour in, both on and off the forum. The trolls came in full force, commenting and messaging me daily. Instagram, Facebook, Twitter, my blog—you name it and they were there, multiple people telling me I looked unkempt and sloppy in my photos, making fun of my bushy eyebrows, and telling me to get off the internet. After a feature celebrating my twenty-five-pound weight loss journey published in *Women's Health*, a prominent magazine and website for women, someone on Facebook accused me of lying.

"Good for her for losing weight, but she doesn't look like the size eight she claims to be," the comment read.

When I was visiting San Francisco for a brand partnership that holiday season, someone I had never met or engaged with online told me to jump off the Golden Gate Bridge while I was in the city.

Comments like these seeped deep into my bones. I wondered if these strangers were right—about everything. I analyzed every Instagram photo I shared and every blog I published to figure out what caused these comments. I reconsidered how I showed up online and what I could change to avoid negativity. In the blink of an eye, I became a filtered version of myself, no longer sharing in-the-moment sweaty selfies but fully curated, high-quality photos taken on my fancy camera. Each comment reinforced the idea I was a failure with no future ahead of me.

On top of this, I was alone most of the day. A few months prior, Matt and I got a notice that our rent was increasing by nearly five hundred dollars per month for our two-bedroom, one-bathroom apartment, close to what was then Sunnyvale's eerily empty downtown. At the time, I worked primarily from home and had the opportunity to work fully remote; I couldn't justify paying that much in rent when I could work anywhere in the world.

The year before, we took the week before Thanksgiving off to go on a road trip from Portland, Oregon, to Seattle, Washington. Neither of us had visited the Pacific Northwest before, but we immediately fell in love. As soon as we arrived and rented our car, Matt drove along Highway 26 to our hotel in Hillsboro. With the fifty-mile-per-hour speed limit, we were literally forced to slow down compared to the eighty miles per hour we typically drove in California, giving me time to absorb the scenery from the passenger seat. On the thirty-minute drive from the airport, we drove through what felt like an urban forest. I looked out in awe, absorbing the dark green trees lining the highway, the lush grass, and the rolling hills in the background. I saw so much *space* compared to the Bay Area.

As we drove further west, highway signs told us we were arriving in Hillsboro.

"We should move here," I said out loud. Although I knew nothing about Oregon, I craved the slower pace that we were already starting to experience.

Matt laughed. "Hold your horses, love. We've only been in Oregon thirty minutes."

Over the next week, we explored different parts of Portland and Seattle, gravitating toward slower life in the suburbs. In each area, we toured a couple apartments to see how the pricing, layout, and feel compared to that of the Bay Area. Rent in Seattle seemed to average just three hundred dollars cheaper per month while we could get a luxury three-bed, two-bath in Portland for less than we were paying per month.

When we got the notice in our mailbox that our rent would be significantly increasing, moving to Portland felt like a no-brainer.

"So this is it?" I asked. "We're really doing this? We're moving to Oregon?"

"We're moving to Oregon," Matt concurred.

"If we hate it," I said, "we can always move to Seattle in a year. Right?"

"Right."

I got approval to work remotely with the same salary, and Matt found a new role within his company that would allow him to work from the Hillsboro satellite office. We called one of the apartments we toured in Tualatin, about thirty minutes outside of downtown Portland, and secured a year-long lease. Three weeks later, we were in a moving truck, driving the twelve hours to our new home where we knew absolutely no one. Our closest family members were no longer a drive away; they were a plane ride and nearly one thousand miles south in a different state. Portland was foreign to us.

Between the loneliness from working at home, the isolation from not having any in-person friends, and the overwhelming online negativity, I sank into a deep funk, questioning everything about who I was. I retreated from loved ones, felt more anxiety than I had ever experienced, and stopped taking care of myself. I typically worked out at least twice a day, one of which was a long walk along a gorgeous river trail, but I couldn't muster the energy. At one point, I didn't work out for six weeks straight. For a fitness lover like me, that was a tell-tale sign something was off.

It scared me to tell anyone how bad it had gotten. I didn't want to burden anyone, especially my loved ones. My mom was heading into her busy season at work, Matt was settling into a new job, and, being new to Oregon, I was alienated from my closest friends.

"When in doubt, call me. No matter what time," my mom had said this repeatedly over the years, more as a gentle reminder than a must-do. She let my brother and me come to her when we were ready, but this would be my first time talking to her, much less anyone, about mental health.

On a chilly January Monday in 2016, I sat bundled up on the couch, my hands shaking in fear. I unlocked my phone, clicked the phone icon, navigated to my favorites, and clicked on "Mom."

"Can you talk?" I asked once she answered.

"Of course," she replied. "I always have time for my favorite daughter."

For the first time in my adult life, I opened up. Not all the way, just a crack.

"I can't do this anymore," I started. I told her how devastated I was by the overwhelmingly negative comments online and explained how frustrated, sad, and lonely I was. I told her I missed her and my dad more than I thought I would. I finished my long-winded monologue by saying, "Mostly, I miss being able to meet you halfway, just to get dinner," through sniffles.

Maybe it was mother's intuition, but she seemed to know the situation was worse than I was letting on, so much so that she insisted we go on a girl's trip as soon as possible.

"We can't go on a trip until after April fifteenth," I reminded her. It was a well-known fact within our family that we didn't travel or make any big plans between January first and April fifteenth, given my mom's busy season at work.

"This is more important," she countered.

On Sunday, January 11, we booked a stay at a wellness resort in Ivins, Utah, that I found online. Just four days later, we met in baggage claim at the Las Vegas airport, her flying in from Monterey and me from Portland, ready to drive the two hours to paradise.

A few minutes after driving down the Vegas Strip, my mom asked if I had ever wanted to visit Vegas. I had been once when I was little but had just one memory of getting violently sick outside of the M&M Store, jealous that my brother and dad got to go in while I had to wait outside as I threw up in the bushes. My brother walked out holding a yellow M&M character that was bigger than he was.

"We wanted to give this to you because you're sick," he told me nicely, handing over the giant stuffed ball.

Ever since then, Vegas became synonymous with the place I got violently ill. I never wanted to go back, scared I'd get as sick as I once did.

"Vegas isn't really my scene," I told my mom. "I don't like the idea of so many drunk people on the streets, and I'm not really into gambling." I paused, thinking. "That said, I have thought about coming for a weekend so I can go to GIADA, eat at Nobu, and see *O*," I told my mom, referring to two famed restaurants and Cirque Du Soleil's aquatic-themed show that I had been itching to see since my mom mentioned it over a decade earlier. "But that's about it."

"Why don't we do those while we're here?" she asked as she navigated into the left lane, aiming to make a U-turn and take us back to the Strip. It was 2:00 p.m.; if we hurried, we could make it to GIADA just before they closed for an afternoon break at 3:00 p.m.

I was giddy as we parked and walked into the lobby of the Cromwell Hotel. I looked up in awe at the giant "GIADA" sign on the wall and asked my mom to take a picture of me standing in front of it. I watched *The Food Network* religiously, and I couldn't *wait* to taste the food of one of the chefs I looked up to on TV.

"We're only seating at the bar and have a limited happy hour menu," the host said in a monotone greeting.

"That's great," my mom replied. "Thank you."

We ordered a pizza to share and I'm sad to admit that it was quite disappointing. I had high hopes but it tasted like any other overpriced pizza. Strike one.

"Want to get Nobu for dinner?" my mom asked as she googled their hours on her phone. "They open at five, and they have one reservation, right when they open. I'm booking it!"

"Are you sure?" I asked. "Nobu's really expensive." We were splitting the cost of the trip, and a five-hundred-dollar dinner wasn't in my budget.

"My treat," she replied. "Just don't tell dad." She winked.

When we finished our snack, we walked through the Cromwell Hotel and across the street to Caesars Palace where Nobu was located. We spent the two hours in between reservations wandering through the myriad of stores in the hotel and playing on the slot machines, my first time legally gambling. At 5:00 p.m. on the dot, we walked into Nobu, not caring how under-dressed we were in our wrinkled t-shirts, jeans and sneakers; we were just excited to have gotten a last-minute reservation.

From the moment we sat down and opened the menu, our mouths started to water. Sushi is my absolute favorite food, and I'd heard Nobu was the best. Unable to decide on what to get, we asked our waitress for a recommendation.

"Do you want me to let the chef decide for you?" she offered. "You can tell me how many dishes you want and they'll send out their favorites."

My mom and I glanced at each other, a silent conversation happening.

"Yes, please," we responded at the same time. We both ate anything and everything and were definitely open to being surprised.

Before we knew it, our table filled with tiny dishes. Paper-thin sashimi. Melt-in-your-mouth black cod miso. Traditional sushi rolls. The highlight of the meal was by far and away the Japanese Wagyu that was cooked table-side on hot stones. It was hands-down the best meal I had ever had.

Full and satisfied, we made our way back to the car and drove the two hours to the resort. At one point in the drive, the mile markers on the freeway reset.

"Does that mean we're almost there?" I asked my mom excitedly, the same feeling washing over me as it did when we got close to the Sierra Mountains for our annual August vacation.

"Maybe? I don't know," My mom admitted. "I'm just following the map."

My phone had no service so I couldn't look up how much longer to go. Twenty minutes later, the mile markers started again.

"I'm so confused," I said out loud, refreshing to see if I had service.

"We just drove through Arizona!" I exclaimed. "And we're just fifteen minutes away!" I hadn't been this excited in months.

The next three and a half days were filled with rest and relaxation. I bought a spa package with a massage, body treatment, facial, manicure, and pedicure, which they allowed me to spread out throughout my stay. Each morning, I went from breakfast to the spa, enjoying my new favorite drink—a Bombay Chai matcha—in the relaxation room overlooking the deep red canyon while I waited for my treatment of the day to begin. After lunch, my mom and I walked the labyrinth, took an afternoon nap, and ate a healthy dinner in their restaurant before calling it a night. Because we were there during the off-season, it felt like we had the entire place to ourselves. The solace was exactly what I needed.

On our last day, after checking out, we drove the opposite direction of the airport to enjoy the red rocks one last time. We parked the car and walked a few hundred yards into an open park, where I pulled out my camera for the first time, wanting to document the trip for Instagram. I asked a woman on the trail to take a photo of us in front of a large rock together. Standing there next to someone I loved in a place full of peace, I smiled for the first time in months.

9

THE TROLLS ARE BACK

I didn't learn my lesson. Just over a year later, I googled myself again.

In early 2017, I had a realization: maybe if my name wasn't tied to my Instagram or blog, it would feel different. Things would be anonymous, the hate comments would stop, and I could post whatever I wanted. On a whim, I changed my Instagram handle and blog name from Lauren Lives Healthy to Wandering in Wellness. By giving myself permission to explore other areas of the industry, I hoped to reset my dwindling online presence.

After overhauling my website and working feverishly to optimize my site for search engines amid the rebrand, I typed "Lauren Lives Healthy" into the search bar to make sure the link to my homepage automatically redirected to wanderinginwellness.com. It did, which was good. Before I could exit out of the tab, my eye caught a familiar-looking link:

Page 135 | Healthy Living Bloggers | Forums, the heading read.

Next to the publish date, April 4, 2017, the snippet read, "Does anyone here follow Lauren Lives Healthy (now Wandering In Wellness rolleyes)? She's a former (?) [program] girl (she's quit and rejoined [program] ..."

My stomach dropped. Before I could help myself, I clicked on the link, leading to the same forum I found the year prior. I found the comment:

> *Does anyone here follow Lauren Lives Healthy (now Wandering In Wellness rolleyes)? She's a former (?) [program] girl (she's quit and rejoined [program] probably 5 times in as many years) with a blog that I think has been talked about here. I actually unfollowed her awhile ago (when she swore off working out for the 100th time) and started posting all kinds of weird "superfood," super high-calorie lattes/smoothies/butters/etc. that I found obnoxious and not helpful.*

It continued on for two more paragraphs, ending with "Time to mooooove on."

Another comment asked if it was time to make a separate thread, which it appeared they had. I clicked over to a page called Wandering in Wellness/Lauren Lives Healthy, a thread dedicated solely to bashing me and only me. Three out of the first five comments read:

> *I need this thread to happen. Especially now that she thinks she's important enough to post a whole thing about how she's #standinguptobullies after reading here. Come on y'all make my dreams come true. hahaha*

> *I'm here and ready to make this thread happen! [Lauren] is my favorite hate read. Her rant about [this site] just made me want to talk about her even more.*

Yes!!! Did you see how many people were boo-hooing with her on her "poor me people are so mean" instagram post?? I think it said like 70 comments. WHAT.

A slew of other comments on the first page agreed that I binge-ate, was extremely inconsistent, overtrained, ranted too much, got too much sympathy, was a hypocrite, essentially sold myself out for sponsorships, and, in general, wasn't healthy like I portrayed on Instagram. Comments like these were front and center:

Other than [Lauren] losing 25 or so pounds doing [a health program] a few years ago, she's done nothing aspirational or worth looking up to. Her approach to wellness and health is a joke and it's clear that she STILL has no idea what she is doing.

She needs to fess up on how she binge eats and smells like a mustard freak.

She's been my favorite source of reverse motivation for at least a year now.

This girl looks like a hot mess. There is nothing about her that I find inspiring. She looks unkempt and sloppy in all of her pictures.

She annoys the hell out of me and for gods sake get your damn eyebrows waxed girl.

It kind of makes me wonder if she is dealing with some
low-grad[e] depression, that she's convinced herself that
sitting in the bathtub so much is a good thing.

...and those were just a selection of the comments from page one. Out of five.

Bile started rising in my throat, making me instantly nauseated. I was already mentally hanging on by a thread, still processing the allure and uncertainty that came with moving to a different state the prior year. I still hadn't made friends in our new city, and my corporate career was on the back burner of the back burner as I started to prepare for my next move. Rumors of another round of layoffs happening in a few short months abounded, and I was confident I would be impacted due to the unique nature of my role. These comments were the cherry on top of the melting sundae. Before long, I fell into an even deeper funk than the first time I found the site. I needed a break, an escape.

As I was scrolling Instagram one day, I came across a platform called 109 World, which used the power of social media to bring together social influencers and everyday folks to make a difference. They hosted social mission trips where volunteers spent a chunk of time on location, supporting grassroots organizations for a specific cause. The nonprofit had built animal shelters in Aruba, brought drinking water to a remote village in Nicaragua, and provided on-the-ground disaster relief efforts after a major earthquake in Ecuador. They were making a difference and I wanted to be a part of it.

The next scheduled trip was supporting children at a refugee camp in Greece, which seemed extremely fitting.

Most, if not all, of my volunteer work related to children in some form or another. In high school, I cofounded a local chapter of an organization that provided lower-income children with shoes, books, and supplies so they could attend school comfortably. In high school, I had the opportunity to travel to Vietnam with my aunt to shadow the adoption experience, visit orphanages, and learn about the poor circumstances in the homes. In my college years, I fundraised and supported St. Jude Children's Research Hospital, which seeks to find cures for children with cancer and other life-threatening diseases. I believed in the power of children, and supporting refugee kids sold me on the trip. I also loved that they weaved sunrise yoga into the daily schedule. The timing couldn't have been more perfect for a trip like this.

Just a few months prior, my company launched a giving-back program where employees could take up to forty hours of paid leave to give back in a way that was personally meaningful. Employees could use the hours to support a local cause a few hours each month, or all at once on a bigger scale, such as attending a volunteer program. The Greece trip fit the bill, making it even more of a draw. As part of registration, I had to fundraise or give approximately three thousand dollars, a large portion of which went directly to the refugee camp as a grant. I created an online fundraising campaign and started saving. Because I'd be flying twenty hours each way, I decided to tack on a week of vacation beforehand to explore the Greek Islands, which I had dreamt of seeing in person for years.

When I arrived in Greece, I stayed one night in Athens before taking a ferry to Santorini. If there's one place you do not want to go on a solo trip, it's a romance-filled island. Everywhere I looked, I saw couples: newlyweds, couples celebrating anniversaries, people on babymoons. I was an outlier everywhere I went.

One morning, I took the hotel concierge's advice to go on a half-day snorkeling tour in and around the caldera. As soon as I stepped in the van, the driver asked if anyone would be joining me.

"Nope, it's just me," I said.

A group of women in the backseat chimed in, "Aw, you poor thing! You can hang out with us today so you're not alone."

The clear, sapphire blue ocean was unlike anything I'd ever seen before. Minus the extremely awkward lobster-red sunburn I got—I wore an intricate one-piece with dozens of crisscrossed lines across the back—those few hours on the Mediterranean Sea were exactly what I needed. The following day, I took a ferry to a tiny island called Folegandros. Upon checking in to my hotel around 2:00 p.m., I was informed that the entire island shut down for a siesta from 2:00 p.m. until around 5:00 p.m. or later. Pulling out a map, the receptionist showed me directions to the main street so I could find dinner later that evening.

"Do you recommend doing anything in particular while I'm here?" I asked. I loved getting recommendations from locals.

"Oh yes," she replied excitedly. "There's a wonderful beach to swim at on the other side of the island. You can either take a taxi or walk along the footpath here," she said, pointing to a thick line on the map. "It's a beautiful view and won't take long," she promised.

Feeling exhausted and jet lagged, I opted to save the walk for the next day and hole up in my room watching TV. During a layover, I splurged and bought all episodes of a popular TV series and wanted to make my way through all five seasons. Guilt poured over me as I realized I could be doing the same thing at home, sixty-four hundred miles away with my dog by my side. Unable to push the thought away, I got up and walked into town to explore, only to return fifteen minutes later. In that time, I walked from my hotel, up and down the main street, and through the winding alleyways. Its size paled in comparison to Santorini.

The next morning, full from a traditional Greek breakfast spread, I set off to find the walking path the receptionist recommended. I looked for a paved path but couldn't find one; instead, I saw a small, rocky trail, just barely big enough to fit one foot in front of the other. *I guess I'm going for a hike rather than a walk*, I thought looking at the mountainous terrain ahead.

Well into the hike, I walked down a steep hill and found myself alone in the middle of a desolate canyon. The trail had a few markers throughout—small rocks guiding the way—but I couldn't for the life of me figure out where the trail continued. I walked along the trench, thinking it may have been part of the hike, only to come to a dead end. I promptly started panicking. I didn't have a map, my phone didn't have service, and I was by myself on what felt like Greece's most isolated island. *What the hell was I thinking, coming here alone?*

As I paced back and forth through the canyon floor, hyperventilating, I spotted something on the ground. When I went to pick it up, a huge breath escaped my mouth. It was a map of the island. I had never felt more relief in my life.

My relief quickly dissipated; the map didn't have the trail marked on it. *Fuck.*

Finally, after about thirty minutes, I saw a couple inching down a steep trail from the side of the canyon I needed to go to. As soon as they made their way down into the canyon and up the other side, I ran over with a sigh of relief and made my way up the hill. Turns out there was a rock marker at the bottom of the trail; I just missed it in my panic.

As soon as I got to the top of the hill, I froze in awe. In front of me was the most beautiful view I had ever seen in my life: a small, calm bay surrounded by jutting black rocks, a stark contrast to the light blue water of the sea. Along the shore, I spotted my destination, a sandy white beach in front of a row of white stucco buildings.

As I started making my way along the rocky path, the sky shifted from clear blue skies to cloudy, and in an instant, rain started pouring down. Carefully but quickly, I ran the rest of the way to the beach, not at all dressed or prepared for the change in weather. I walked into one of the buildings, a seafood restaurant, to see if I could wait out the rain, but they were closed until dinner. A run-down bus stop sat just down the road, so I ran over to stand under the small awning. A few minutes later, an unmarked van pulled up.

"Are you going to the other side of the island?" a young woman yelled through the window.

"Yes." I nodded, unsure if I should ask for a ride or wait it out.

"I'm heading there now," she said. "Do you want a ride? The buses aren't running today."

Drenched and uncomfortable, I decided to risk being murdered instead of trying to make my way back along what I imagined would now be a very muddy trail. I hopped in the front seat and off we went, stopping a few minutes later to pick up another stray who was also caught in the rain. The woman told us that it very rarely rained on the island and this was a special occasion. As she drove, she explained she was a local tour guide during the summer, pointing out some of her favorite places and relaying the island's history during our five-minute drive. She dropped each of us off at our respective hotels and refused to take anything but a wave in return for her kindness.

"We're a family here," she said. "We help each other out."

I learned more about myself on that island—and specifically that hike—more than the rest of the trip combined, which is saying a lot given the nature of the retreat. Sitting in my bed watching Netflix, I realized I never truly give myself permission to slow down. It's okay, I learned, to do so, no matter where I am in the world. Getting lost on that trail and finding my way back—both on my own in a foreign country—helped me feel confident in a way I had never felt before. Missing the trail marker was a reminder to slow down and look around before panicking. The instant shift in weather reminded me that everything can change in the blink of an eye, and I can handle whatever's thrown my way. The kindness of a stranger restored my faith in humanity. Overall, I learned that there was so much more than life on the internet.

The best part of all? I didn't document any of this on social media, so no one knew what happened on that trail except for me. It was my little secret—at least for a little while.

10

LOVING AND LOSING
MY SOULMATE

On August 1st, 2017, just weeks after I returned from Greece, Gigi died in my arms.

Gigi was a ten-pound Shih Tzu I rescued in the summer of 2011 from the Monterey Society for the Prevention of Cruelty to Animals when she was five years old. She was, without a doubt, the greatest love of my life.

Growing up, my dad and I went on weekend dates to the shelter to pet and walk the dogs. We'd wander along the rows of kennels and give attention to every single stray. We'd pick one dog to walk around the property, and after getting permission from the volunteers, we'd put a leash on them, leave the building, and meander through the parking lot, watching the dog experience freedom beyond the four walls of its cage.

Whenever I was home from college, my dad and I visited the shelter, reliving our father-daughter dates as grown-ups. One weekend, we spontaneously drove the fifteen minutes to the SPCA, ready to spend the afternoon loving on animals that weren't our own. Like always, we walked up and down the room of cages, petting and talking to each dog individually. Many of the dogs barked and jumped when we gave them extra attention. Not Gigi. Gigi hid in the corner of her kennel with her booty backed as far up against the wall as she could get. I sat on the floor outside of her cage and coaxed her toward me, sensing that all she needed was a little extra love.

I asked to take her into a playroom, thinking that was more her style than a walk outside. Inside the small visiting room, my dad sat on the bench while I sat on the floor, with Gigi hovering on the complete opposite side of the room. It took twenty minutes for her to make her way over to me. She'd take a step forward before taking three steps back. At one point, she was so scared she peed on the floor. I coaxed her around the small puddle, eventually bribing her to come close enough to me that I could gently pet her head.

A few minutes later, a volunteer took Gigi back to her cage while my dad and I headed home. Unlike the other dogs who drifted from my mind before we arrived back at the house, I couldn't stop thinking about Gigi and her brown puppy dog eyes. I wasn't in the market for a dog, but I fell in love with her that day.

During my three-day visit, my dad and I went back to the shelter every afternoon to give Gigi some much-needed attention. Each day on the drive over, I told him how sad I would be if she wasn't there.

"That would be a good sign," he reminded me. "Her not being there would mean someone took her home."

To my delight, she was there each time we returned.

Over the next three days, Gigi started to warm up to me. When I kneeled down in front of her kennel, holding the back of my hand flat against the cage so she could smell me, she walked toward me without shaking. She no longer peed on the floor when we sat in the playroom, and she let me take her on walks around the property. Slowly but surely, she was coming out of her shell.

As an older dog, we knew it would take longer for her to find a home than a puppy. On the last day of my trip, my dad asked if today was the day I was going to adopt her, knowing I wouldn't be able to come back to the shelter in the following days or weeks after returning to school.

"I'm in college," I reminded him—and myself. "I can't get a dog."

I was a rising junior who, during the school year, had two jobs on top of a full workload. I was subletting an apartment for the summer, unsure of where I'd be living come fall. How would I have time to care for a dog? I had no idea, but I saw it in her eyes: Gigi needed me as much as I needed her. My dad offered to pay the one-hundred-dollar adoption fee, and I signed the adoption forms without hesitation. Once we were approved to leave, I led her to the car, both of us nervous yet eager to start our new life together. As soon as we got home, my mom took us to PetSmart to get the necessities: a leash, a bed, food, treats, and even a few toys in hopes she would play with them. Turns out, she didn't like toys; she preferred to sleep in her spare time.

The next day, I drove the two hours back to my apartment, Gigi sitting in the front seat beside me.

"We'll figure this out together," I promised her.

True to my word, we made it through the rest of the summer with no major incidents.

After living in a sorority house the previous year, I was ready to live alone. I chose to rent a studio apartment a short walk from campus. Not ready to move in together, my boyfriend-at-the-time got a separate studio on the same floor, just a few doors down.

On the day we moved in, my parents came to help. The apartment was furnished, so there wasn't really much to move. After spending a couple of hours unpacking and organizing my stuff, we spent the rest of the two days teaching Gigi how to stay alone in the apartment in anticipation of my busy school days ahead.

For breakfast, my parents and I had lox and bagels, a family favorite. After cleaning up, we went out for a short walk, giving Gigi a few minutes to acclimate to the apartment on her own. We came back to the salmon packaging torn up and strewn across the floor.

Later that night, we went out for dinner, eager to see how Gigi would do at home alone for a longer period of time. Unsure of leaving her in the whole apartment after that morning's incident, we chose to leave her in the bathroom for the hour or so we were gone. When we came back, every inch of paint along the bottom two inches of the bathroom door was completely scratched off and the toilet paper roll was shredded to bits, covering the entire bathroom floor.

"Well," I told my parents, "I guess she has a little separation anxiety."

"It's okay," my mom cooed to Gigi. "We don't mind the mess. Do we?"

Because I lived and worked within a one-mile radius, it was the perfect setup. I could run home in between classes or on a break at work, walk Gigi, and spend time with her. Before long, we found our own rhythm, getting more and more comfortable with each other as the days passed.

Eventually, it got to the point where I could take her to the small park behind our building without her leash on. After doing her business, she'd typically rush back up the six flights of stairs, eager to get back to either my or my boyfriend's third-floor apartment, whichever room we left from.

Early on in the quarter, a graduate student moved into the unit right below me. Like others in the building, we had gotten into a routine of waving and saying hi when we saw each other in the hallways but didn't have much of a rapport beyond that. He often left his door open so he and a friend who lived next door could walk in and out at their leisure.

One afternoon, after my neighbor lived there for just a few days, I took Gigi out for her typical off-leash walk to the park. Instead of running back up the four half-flights of stairs when we returned, she stopped at two. She took off and ran straight into his room, jumped up on his bed, and lay right down. Within seconds, she'd made herself at home.

"Gigi!" I yelled, running straight to her.

I turned around in embarrassment as I realized I just full-on intruded into someone's home and living space in the same way my dog had thirty seconds prior.

"Oh my god, I'm so sorry. I can't believe I just did that. That she just did that. I'm so sorry. I'm so embarrassed. I live right above you. Maybe she thought this was our apartment since it has the same setup and furniture as mine? Again, I'm so sorry," I stuttered.

"Honestly," he said amidst a laugh, "it's fine. I love dogs. Don't worry."

Gigi had no care in the world. It seemed her sole purpose in life was to give and receive love, exactly what I needed as I was navigating a toxic, codependent relationship, planning for the future, and preparing to start a new life in the Bay Area.

In my research about Shih Tzus, I learned the "lion dog" originated in Tibet, where they were bred to be lap warmers for emperors and their families. According to the American Kennel Club, it wasn't until the 1930s that people outside of royalty started owning the breed. Living up to the Shih Tzu stereotype, Gigi was a lap dog who loved nothing more than following me from room to room. I had begun to call her Velcro because she never left my side.

At the end of a long day, I could count on Gigi to welcome me home with kisses and love, something I craved but hadn't received in my human relationships. She comforted me when I felt alone and loved me when I believed no one else did. She saved me just as much as I saved her.

Even though we didn't speak the same language, we had full conversations together. When something happened, big or small, she was often the first one I told. I talked to her about anything and everything with no filter, the same way I'd talk to a friend.

"Guess what?" I'd ask as soon as I walked in the door, even before putting my backpack or groceries down.

You know the drill, she'd remind me with a nuzzle on my legs. *Love first and then we can talk.*

Just seconds after I not-so-gracefully fell backward on the couch, she'd jump up on my lap and give me hundreds of kisses. With her, love came first. Always.

I didn't believe in soulmates, but something in me changed when I met Gigi. She was the only being in the world I could be my true self with. Unlike my other relationships, we had no judgment between us. I felt truly and utterly at home with her. When I looked into her eyes, I felt like we knew everything about each other, a feeling I was confident she reciprocated.

When I met my now-husband, I joked that he had to get approval from Gigi before we could officially start dating.

"You say that with a laugh," he said with a chuckle, "but I know you're not joking. I know where I stand." Although he quickly became the second love of my life, Matt knew from the get-go that he would always be second to Gigi.

In the six years we had together, Gigi and I went through so many big and small moments together: turning twenty-one, graduating college, moving to the Bay Area, starting my first "real" job, falling in love with my husband, moving to Oregon. In our final few months together, though, everything spiraled out of control.

At the time, we lived in a townhouse in Hillsboro, a suburb of Portland. The three-story space was thin and tall, with no way to avoid the flight of stairs that led from the entry way up to the living area. A second set of carpeted stairs led from the dining area up to the bedrooms.

One day, Gigi tripped down the second set of stairs, landing clumsily yet softly on the carpet near the dining room. She slipped on the last step, which wasn't a rare occurrence for any of us, so I didn't think much of it. I went to Greece as planned. During one of our daily conversations, Matt told me that she yelped when he picked her up, but that was the extent of her discomfort. We thought that, perhaps, she hurt her leg when she fell, but we didn't think too much of it.

When I got home, things seemed to be okay, but the yelping continued to happen off-and-on every few days. Not sure what was happening, we took her to the vet for an exam. Nothing showed up in the blood tests or x-rays, but they gave us a preventative antibiotic and Gabapentin to help the pain.

After two more weeks, she was acting even more unlike herself, despite finishing both rounds of medications. We went back to the vet, who urged us to make an appointment with a pet neurologist. I had never heard of a pet neurologist before, but I would have done anything for Gigi, so we drove over an hour to the closest specialist for a secondary x-ray, MRI, and a series of other tests as soon as possible.

"I'm sorry," the doctor told us during the report-out. "I've never seen anything like this before. It looks like a disease is eating away at the tissue around her spine, but I can't identify what it is. It's a mystery, even to me." The specialist sent us home with a six-thousand-dollar bill and no answers.

Gigi quickly deteriorated. Within three days, she wasn't even able to stand up high enough off the ground to urinate. With every deep look into my eyes, she told me she was suffering. I called the vet in tears, telling them she had gotten worse.

"I think it's time," our vet told us. "I can't tell you what to do, but if she's unable to go to the bathroom, I can tell you without a doubt she's in a lot of pain." We made a euthanasia appointment for three days later.

In an effort to give Gigi the best experience possible, we committed to doing all of her favorite things in those final days. On Sunday, we drove ninety minutes each way to Cannon Beach, Oregon, so she could feel sand on her paws. Although she wasn't able to run or even walk on the beach, we wanted to take her somewhere that reminded her of Carmel Beach, one of her favorite places, which we went to anytime we were visiting my parents.

On her last day, a Tuesday, Matt and I both took the day off work. In deciding how to spend her last hours, we thought she would want nothing more than to be with her two favorite humans. It was a clear day, the temperature hovering at seventy-five degrees, so we stopped by the grocery store for sandwiches and picked a random park on the map where we could enjoy a picnic. After twenty-five minutes, we arrived at a secluded park that had little more than a picnic bench overlooking the Tualatin Valley. Despite the perfect weather, I spent the entire morning hugging her, silent tears spilling into her white and gray fur.

We arrived at the vet's office a few minutes before our 2:00 p.m. appointment.

"Do you want to be in the room with her?" the vet tech asked.

Not really, I replied in my head. Instead, "Yes, please," came out of my mouth.

Clutching her to my chest, we followed the tech into the furthest exam room, set slightly apart from the others.

"I'm so sorry," our vet said as she walked into the room. She was our favorite vet at the clinic, and I special-requested that she was the one in the room for this appointment. I sat in the chair, just barely loosening my grip so Gigi could lie down on my lap and rest her head on my forearm. The vet explained what would happen, but I couldn't focus through my tears. After giving Gigi a sedative for comfort, the vet gave us a few minutes alone to say goodbye while it took effect. A quick knock rang through the room seconds before the vet re-entered.

"It's time," she said, tears filling her eyes.

As she gave the final injection, I hunched over Gigi's body, sobbing harder than I ever had in my life. I gasped loudly, trying to breathe through the tears that were running down my face at an immeasurable rate. My body shook uncontrollably, bawling as I felt Gigi's breaths slow.

She was facing away from me, so all I could see was her right ear, nose, and the side of her face. I avoided her eyes, knowing I would feel even more guilt upon seeing the fear in her brown eyes. Watching the vet reach up to close her eyes caused me to sob even harder. The vet gently took her limp body from me, saying that someone would contact us within a few weeks to pick up her ashes.

When we walked out of the room, we saw candles lit with signs that asked all patients in the waiting room to be quiet and respectful as a fellow pet owner was saying goodbye. I thought I was out of tears, but they came back, falling down my face faster than before.

Without a doubt, this was the hardest moment of my life. Although I knew her end was coming, I never said goodbye—not really. For years after her death, I walked around in a stupor clouded with shame, anger, and resentment, convinced the hole in my heart would never be repaired. Because I didn't go into depth on my feelings and emotions, you'd never know from looking at my Instagram feed how much I was struggling, trying to stay afloat in a current that kept pulling me out to sea.

11

FINALLY, A DIAGNOSIS (OR TWO)

On top of losing and grieving Gigi, I was struggling on the health front.

During high school, despite working out hours a day and becoming more aware of my diet, I felt extreme exhaustion, lethargy, and weakness. After years of these complaints and no guidance from our family doctor, my mom took me to an out-of-network functional medicine doctor to see if we could figure out the issue. The doctor ran several blood tests, concluding that my thyroid gland wasn't producing enough hormones, an issue called hypothyroidism.

"What does that mean?" my mom asked curiously.

"It means that Lauren will have to be on medication the rest of her life," the doctor replied.

After discussing the different treatment options—an extensive collection of natural medication and herbal supplements—my mom and I walked out of the office empty-handed. Confused, I asked my mom why we didn't try them.

"I'm not paying two hundred dollars a month for medication," she replied, her voice fraught with annoyance. "That's absolutely ridiculous." She looked over at me with an eye roll.

I didn't understand. My mom splurged on vacations, handbags, and expensive meals without hesitation; why not something the doctor recommended that could help me feel better?

"Let's talk to another doctor," she recommended. "Get a second opinion."

I crossed my arms in front of my chest and slouched back into the passenger seat. I understood her reasoning, but I didn't *want* to go to another doctor. I liked this one and she had a solution.

A few weeks later, we walked into the office of a highly recommended internist in Monterey. After confirming the diagnosis, the doctor agreed I would have to be on medication for the rest of my life. The good news? There was a synthetic option I could take that was covered by my parents' insurance, and it was a fraction of the price of the previously prescribed supplements.

"It's the only change you'll have to make," promised the doctor. "As long as you take one of these pills every morning, your symptoms will go away and you can live life like a normal teenager."

Taking that little white pill became the reason I woke up in the morning—literally; I had to take it on an empty stomach thirty minutes before ingesting anything other than water. I never missed a day. Ever. Not when I woke up early for a swim meet, not when we were visiting family in San Francisco, and not during our annual summer trip to the mountains. Everywhere I went, that bright orange prescription bottle was in my purse or backpack.

Even though I took the medication religiously, my symptoms lingered. I was freezing year-round, wearing the same thick sweatshirt in winter and during the dead of the summer. My muscles felt weak, my joints were constantly aching, and my hair fell out at an abnormal rate. Worst of all was the never-ending fatigue. Even if I got a solid eight hours of sleep, I moved slowly throughout the day and struggled to keep up with the pace of school, work, relationships, and life.

In my third year of college, four years after starting the thyroid medication, I started feeling sick after every single meal. Regardless of whether I ate a sandwich from the cafeteria, a frozen pizza, or a salad, I felt nauseated within twenty minutes of eating. Don't even get me started on alcohol; after just a couple sips, my stomach would churn uncomfortably.

Not wanting to burden my friends or boyfriend-at-the-time, I rarely mentioned when I felt sick, instead riding out the symptoms on my own. If I was out in public or with someone else, I'd excuse myself and run to the bathroom, where I could breathe through the worst of the discomfort in peace.

As I had growing up, I turned to food as my source of comfort. Whenever I felt frustrated with my body, often multiple times a day, I'd take myself to my favorite restaurants in between classes, ordering full meals as a pre-meal appetizer. I'd hide the evidence—the pizza box, the crumbs of a clam chowder bread bowl, or the burrito wrapper—before driving home and asking my ex what was for dinner. I ignored the stomach pains after each meal, hoping they would go away on their own.

One night, at home in the comfort of my studio apartment, I suddenly collapsed on the floor, curling into a ball and wrapping my hands around my belly as I breathed through the most intense side pain I had ever experienced. This was on a different level than the stomach pains I felt after each meal; it was like someone pushed a pitchfork into the area under my right rib cage and was twisting nonstop, testing to see how much pain I could handle.

My ex simply stood above me in awe, unsure of what to do. I couldn't form any words to explain what was happening; all I could do was whimper in pain as I waited for the discomfort to pass. When the pain subsided to a manageable level, I called my dad, our unofficial family doctor, for advice.

"Next time it happens," he said, "go to urgent care."

My dad never encouraged me to go to urgent care, much less the emergency room, so I knew this was serious. A few weeks later, the sudden, unbearable pain happened again. Because it was late at night, well after urgent care closed, I opted to manage the pain myself. Once again, I curled up on the floor and put every ounce of energy I had into breathing through the pain and sighing deeply when I could comfortably breathe again.

I went to urgent care the next morning. The doctor ordered labs and an ultrasound, but nothing showed up on the scan.

"Next time it happens, go to the emergency room," the urgent care doctor recommended. "If you go when the pain is happening, they'll have a better chance of figuring out what's happening."

Every few months, the pain hit, but I never followed the doctor's advice. My only memories of the hospital were serious cases: when we had to take my brother in after getting bitten by a dog, my white dress soaked in blood from trying to help contain the wound, and seeing my dad after he had his gallbladder removed. I reasoned a short-lived pain in my abdomen was nothing compared to what either of them went through. I was too scared to go to the emergency room, so I never went. Plus, by the time the most intense pain subsided—within a minute or two—I wouldn't have gotten to the hospital in time for the doctors to see the pain in action. Instead, I rode out the pain at home each time it hit. To this day, they haven't found the source of the pain, despite years of tests, scans, and, yes, even ER visits.

In 2013, after graduating from college, moving to the Bay Area, and completely overhauling my diet as part of the women's health program, I felt healthy for the first time in my life. I was still feeling nauseated after each meal, but for the first time ever, I had the energy to train for and complete triathlons and other road races. Eating well and working out excessively clearly agreed with my system.

Armed with the freedom of having my own generous health insurance plan, thanks to my marketing role at a high-tech company, I found an endocrinologist, a thyroid specialist, to confirm my dosages were correct. Until that point, I had only worked with primary care doctors and internists, but I wanted a specialist's opinion. Their advice wasn't at all what I expected. The doctor recommended I go off all medication, including thyroid medication, birth control, and supplements.

"The other doctors have all told me I have to be on the thyroid medication my whole life," I explained.

"I know," she said. "Your levels are perfect now, though, so it's fine. Going off birth control and other supplements will help reset your system completely." I questioned her recommendation but didn't think to get a second opinion; I trusted the MD at the end of her name.

Within a few months, the symptoms I felt before—exhaustion, lethargy, and muscle weakness—returned, along with severe sensitivity to cold, hair loss, arthritic-like joint pain, and other seemingly unrelated symptoms like heart palpitations. My body went into a complete tailspin, taking me from someone who escaped from Alcatraz and finished half marathons to someone who could barely function in a few short weeks.

By this point, Matt and I had started seriously considering moving to Oregon, so I waited to find a new doctor. I didn't trust the endocrinologist who took me off all medications, and it made sense to find a new set of doctors once we relocated. From experience, I knew it would take months, if not years, to get me back to the healthy, energetic person I was a year prior.

Thinking back to my experience with the naturopath in high school who initially identified my hypothyroidism, I started by making an appointment with a functional medicine doctor. I hoped they would look at my body as a whole, a stark contrast to the experiences I had with Western-trained specialists. Unfortunately, functional medicine wasn't covered by my insurance, but I figured it would be worth the out-of-pocket cost for a few sessions.

We spent our first appointment doing a deep-dive into my symptoms. At my second appointment, we took blood for an initial round of tests. At my third appointment, we did more blood tests and a series of food intolerance tests, wondering if food was the culprit of my mysterious pain. At my fourth appointment, I had a diagnosis.

"You have Hashimoto's," the doctor told me. "You also have hidden Celiac disease, which is really common in Hashimoto's patients. Basically, what that means is that Celiac doesn't show up on tests, but your body reacts to gluten the same way people with Celiac do."

I recognized the term Hashimoto's from my Google searches on hypothyroidism, but I didn't know anything about it other than it was an autoimmune disease. Celiac, on the other hand, I was intimately familiar with. One of my roommates my sophomore year of college had it, and we shared many gluten-free meals before eating gluten free was a popular trend. I knew to avoid anything with wheat, barley, or rye in the ingredient list.

The doctor finished our appointment by saying, "Just continue taking your thyroid pill, add in the supplements we discussed, stop eating gluten, dairy, soy, eggs, and pork, and you'll be good to go."

"What am I supposed to eat?" I asked dumbfounded. Everything I consumed had at least one of those things in it.

"I'll give you some recipes," she replied. "You'll be fine." I looked up in shock and disappointment; I was paying for her expertise, and that was all I got? I wanted her to give me a roadmap—books to read, cookbooks to buy, and resources to dig into; heck, even a pamphlet to take home—but instead, I got a print-out with three basic recipes on it.

I walked out of her office feeling conflicted. Part of me was relieved that I had an official diagnosis, something to explain the majority of symptoms I felt. At the same time, I was frustrated by her lack of explanation, still having no understanding of what Hashimoto's meant. I was also sorely disappointed in her "you'll be fine" approach. I wasn't fine, and the future we discussed didn't look fine, either.

On the way home, I stopped at the naturopathic pharmacy the receptionist recommended to pick up the list of supplements my doctor prescribed. After loading up my cart with Adrenal Complex and a handful of other supplements I couldn't pronounce, I smirked to myself. Now I completely understood my mom's hesitation in the first naturopath's office. The supplements were *ridiculously* expensive.

Back in the car, I called my dad for advice. "Aren't you near one of Oregon's top hospitals?" he asked before encouraging me to see an endocrinologist. Based on my last experience with an endocrinologist, I had my doubts but followed his advice anyway.

As soon as I got home, I looked up Oregon Health and Science's University to see if they had an endocrinology clinic. To my relief, they did. I booked the first appointment, scheduled for four months later. Desperate for answers, I asked to do blood tests in advance so I could review my results in person at our first appointment instead of receiving a diagnosis via a secure online portal. Although it was out of the ordinary, they agreed to my request.

On the day of my appointment, I sat in the waiting room, shaking. I was nervous and giddy, hopeful the endocrinologist would have a life-changing treatment plan for me to implement. As soon as he took my weight, height, and blood pressure, he brought up my labs and we dove right in.

"Your labs confirm you have Hashimoto's," he said. My shoulders tensed, my back now perfectly straight. I knew that was coming, but the shock still hit me like a pile of bricks.

"How do you treat it?" I asked nervously, anticipating the same nonchalant answer I always received.

"Continue taking your thyroid medication every day on an empty stomach," he replied, just as I expected. At that, he stood up, abruptly ending the session.

"Do I need to make any dietary changes?" I asked as I picked up my purse. I wasn't ready for more changes but wanted his opinion, curious how it compared to the cut-everything-out diet the functional medicine doctor prescribed.

"All you have to avoid is gluten," he replied. "I don't know why, but it's shown to make a difference for people with Hashimoto's. Even with pizza, make sure it's not cooked on the same surface as regular dough."

I knew why. After not receiving the answers I hoped for from the functional medicine doctor, I spent every free moment researching Hashimoto's, Celiac, and the relationship between the two while I waited for this appointment. According to my go-to source, the Mayo

Clinic, Hashimoto's disease is a condition in which your immune system attacks your thyroid, a small gland at the base of your neck. The thyroid is a butterfly-shaped gland that affects all aspects of your metabolism and other vital functions, including body temperature and heart rate.

No wonder I'm freezing all the time, I thought.

I also learned why so many Hashimoto's patients struggle with hidden Celiac. Like Hashimoto's, Celiac is an autoimmune disease. When people with Celiac eat gluten, a protein found in wheat, barley, and rye, it causes long-term damage to the lining of their small intestine. Because thyroid proteins look and act similarly to gluten, sometimes Hashimoto's patients experience Celiac-like symptoms when they eat gluten, even if they test negative for Celiac.

Could gluten be the cause of my post-meal nausea? I wondered. When my college roommate so much as touched gluten, she was sick for days. We had to be extremely careful not to use the same pans, dishes, utensils, or cutting boards so she could cook and eat in a Celiac-safe environment. I never connected that my symptoms were a similar, albeit less violent, version of hers.

Learning the science behind it and having a specialist confirm the diagnosis was the driving force I needed to fully eliminate gluten from my diet. I couldn't risk it. I was still struggling to eliminate dairy and soy, but I called it a win that I finally committed to eating gluten-free after months of struggling to give up many of my favorite foods, including bread, pasta, and fried appetizers.

After a few weeks, I started feeling a little better after meals. Thankfully, the unbearable nausea was almost gone, though it was replaced with diarrhea, gas, and bloating within twenty minutes of eating. After finishing a meal, I looked and felt six months pregnant within the hour and had to rush to the bathroom. I assumed it was related to lactose intolerance, so I attempted to eliminate dairy on top of gluten, which felt impossible. After a few weeks, even without both triggers in my system, I noticed massive headaches start to appear after meals, on top of some of the existing symptoms. With every dietary change I experimented with, I went from one gastrointestinal issue to the next—and the more foods I eliminated, the more restricted I felt. In the end, I only seriously committed to eating gluten free. It felt more feasible than eliminating gluten, dairy, soy, eggs, and pork and allowed me to feel like I could still enjoy our restaurant-heavy lifestyle without making everything from scratch.

Although I had the two diagnoses, confirmed by an endocrinologist, I still had a few mysterious symptoms that didn't align with Hashimoto's, Celiac, or my other gastrointestinal issues, namely the gut-wrenching side pain and always-present heart palpitations.

Determined to figure out what was wrong, I went on a wild goose chase from urgent care to primary care to specialist, repeating the same spiel about my history of hypothyroidism and my two autoimmune diagnoses.

"The side pain is unbearable," I'd tell the doctor, nearly in tears from frustration after repeating this same dialogue for what felt like the hundredth time. At each appointment, the nurse would ask in their initial meeting, and then the doctor would repeat the same questions when they came in the room.

"Tell me why you're here today," they'd say.

"I have extreme side pain on my right side that keeps coming back," I'd respond, pointing at the area where it hurts.

"How long does it last for?"

"The intense, can't-breathe-through-it pain lasts for just a few minutes, maybe one or two, but then it's sore and aggravated for about twenty-four hours after."

"What does the pain feel like?"

"Like someone is sticking a pitchfork under my ribs and twisting, digging deeper and pressing harder with each twist."

"Where does the pain happen?"

"I just told you," I'd say exasperated. "My right side. If you'd like I can point you to the exact spot where it hurts. It's always the same place." I'd poke my own side, feeling around until I felt a tender spot.

As soon as the doctor pressed down, I'd wince in pain.

It was the same experience with multiple doctors in different specialties. At each appointment, the doctor would prescribe a round of blood tests along with an ultrasound and/or CAT scan, undoubtedly leaving me with a thousand-dollar-plus bill after insurance with no answers. Regardless of their specialty, the answer was always the same: "I'm sorry. The tests show nothing wrong. Maybe it was a fluke."

After visiting urgent care three times in one week for the side pain, I received a simple update via email: *Good news! Your abdominal ultrasound looks normal. No issue with your liver or gallbladder and the other visualized organs were normal.* There wasn't even a way for me to send a response, asking for what to do next.

Each time I heard a version of this message, my blood boiled. I was sick of missing work to drive an hour to and from Portland for appointments every other week. I hated watching my bank account dwindle, spending my hard-earned paycheck on copays, invoices, and bills instead of vacations and trips back to Carmel to visit family. I was *done* going back and forth with my primary care doctor to get separate referrals for each specialist. I fought with the insurance company time and time again whenever they sent a letter saying they wouldn't cover the scans and medication my doctors prescribed, months after I had already taken the tests and bought the medications. I was frustrated each and every time I was dismissed, made to feel like I was making the pain up, even though both of my partners had seen me bowled-over in pain on regular occasions. I was tired of advocating for myself.

At one of my many doctor's appointments, something unusual happened. When checking my heart rate, the doctor found it running unusually slow—thirty-eight beats per minute compared to my average sixty. The doctor hurried out of the room and, within seconds, returned wheeling in an electrocardiogram (ECG) machine. She attached dozens of electrodes to my body and ran a test to confirm everything was okay with my heart. As always, it showed nothing.

"It's probably a one-time thing," the doctor said as she removed the sensors from my body. "I'm referring you to a cardiologist just in case."

Great, I thought. *Another specialist. Add it to the list.*

When I showed up to my cardiology appointment a few months later, they fitted me with a Holter monitor, a small heart-rate monitor, that I had to wear for seven days without taking it off. I couldn't get it wet, so showers were out of the question. Each time I felt heart palpitations, I had to press a button on the monitor. It was a tedious process that I couldn't ignore. I felt heart palpitations all day every day, and they said this monitor would track those and compare it to when I pressed the button. I wanted to catch each and every palpitation that happened so they could get an accurate view.

"With the exception of one minor skip throughout the week, it looks like your heart rate is normal," the doctor explained at my appointment to remove the monitor. "Sometimes people experience phantom heart palpitations, which may be what's happening in your case."

Tears pricked my eyes and my mind started racing as I realized what he was saying: *phantom, meaning that the heart palpitations are in my head.*

"I'm not saying you're crazy," he clarified, like he was reading my mind. "All I'm saying is that maybe your body thinks your heart is skipping a beat when it really isn't."

Once again, I left a doctor's office feeling frustrated and confused. This time, though, I was convinced that, on top of the physical issues associated with my autoimmune diseases, I was mentally ill.

12

ALWAYS AND FOREVER

The lows of my never-ending health journey were offset by my strong relationship with Matt. After work each evening, we went for a stroll along the Tualatin River before settling in to watch *Jeopardy!* and *Wheel of Fortune* while we ate dinner. Each weekend, we drove into Portland to try a new restaurant, explore a new-to-us neighborhood, or hike Forest Park.

"Do you want to go on a weekend trip?" I asked Matt one evening.

I had been craving time away from my all-in-one living and working situation and kept looking up weekend getaways near Portland. One place in particular, the Columbia River Gorge, stood out to me.

"Sure," Matt said. "Let's do it."

On the Friday of Memorial Day, we left work early to drive the sixty miles to the luxury bed and breakfast I booked. We sat through bumper-to-bumper traffic on the way through Portland. About forty-five minutes into our drive, we saw a sign that read, "Welcome to the Columbia River Gorge."

Within seconds, we saw the most breathtaking view. The deep blue river glistened in the sun and was flanked by a small highway on each side. To our right were thousands upon thousands of trees that seemed to cover every visible inch, except for the few spots in the jutting rock that had little waterfalls, starting hundreds of feet above the ground. To our left, across the river, we could spot the tip of a few of Washington's prominent mountains.

"Want to stop at Multnomah Falls?" I asked Matt.

According to the road signs, we'd be passing the historic waterfall in a few miles, and it seemed like a good place to stretch our legs and let Gigi out.

"Sure," Matt said, navigating into the left lane, preparing to get off at the rapidly approaching exit.

After parking the car and putting Gigi's leash on, we walked through a pedestrian tunnel to get to Oregon's tallest waterfall.

"I'm getting soaked!" I yelled over the booming sound of the waterfall.

"Me too!" Matt shouted back.

"Want to walk up?" I asked, pointing at a little bridge, a ways up the falls. A sign said it was a quarter-mile walk to the bridge, and 2.2 miles to the top of the falls. I walked off before he could answer, knowing he and Gigi would be close behind.

We followed a line of tourists up the small set of switchbacks, arriving at a small bridge a few minutes later. From that angle, the massive waterfall sprayed us even more. I couldn't help but laugh at how unprepared we were. We crossed the bridge and started walking up the path to see where it led. Within seconds, I was completely winded, the steep elevation catching me off-guard.

I looked up to see people at seemingly every switchback doubled over, their hands on their knees as they tried to catch their breath. *Nope.* This was definitely not happening today.

"Let's go back," I told Matt. "We still have a bit of a drive to the B&B."

Google Maps told us it would be thirty minutes to the property, so we piled in the car yet again, ready for the second half of our drive. I took the wheel this time, offering to give Matt a chance to soak in the stunning views.

"You have arrived," my phone announced.

"No we haven't," I muttered. I couldn't tell where it wanted me to turn.

"Do you see the entrance?" I asked Matt.

"I think you drove past it," he replied. "Maybe it was where that sign was?" He pointed behind us.

I made a U-turn, turned past the camouflage sign, and followed the long gravel pathway to an empty lot. We were the only car.

"I'll go check us in," I offered.

"Cool," he said as he put Gigi's leash out. "I'll take her for a short walk."

When I walked into the lodge, I was welcomed by a kind woman, who told me she and her husband were the owners of the property. We bonded over the fact that they were originally from Colorado, as was Matt. She went on to explain that they bought the property in hopes of creating a Pacific Northwest haven for guests to enjoy.

"We'll have homemade breakfast for you in the morning," she said. "Are there any dietary needs I should be aware of?"

"Yes, actually," I said shyly. "I'm gluten free." I still wasn't comfortable asking for people to make exceptions for me.

"Is that something you'd be able to accommodate?" I asked.

"Oh, of course!" she replied instantly. "I was planning to make breakfast burritos tomorrow. I can make you a frittata or something instead; no problem whatsoever."

"I appreciate that so much," I said, thanking her for her generosity.

I got the key to our standalone cabin, which was just on the other side of the parking lot. After unloading the car, we walked over to the cabin to find the front porch complete with a rustic, wooden swing and a quaint bistro table looking out over the property's meadow. Inside was a rustic setup with a king-size bed, a table, a cozy gas fireplace, and a jacuzzi tub.

We dropped off our bags and left to explore the property. They had a meadow in the back with trails just for guests to walk along. The paths were beautifully lined with flowers and plants, a stunning oasis in the middle of a sleepy Washington town.

These cabins became a home away from home over the next few years. Each spring, we booked a weekend away to enjoy the solace and get an escape from the hustle and bustle of our daily lives.

As we prepared for our third visit in 2018, Matt was acting strange. He refused to put his backpack in the trunk with the rest of our luggage, and he insisted that I drive. We put on a playlist and sang along to Death Cab for Cutie, Twenty One Pilots, Vance Joy and other mutual favorites. He refused to look at me the entire drive; instead, he focused intently on tinkering with a piece of paper he found on the floor of my front seat.

"Are you okay?" I asked more than once.

"Yeah, totally."

Guess that's that, I thought.

An hour later, I asked again. "Everything okay, love?"

"Yeah, I'm good."

"I don't believe you," I replied with a smile. I had a feeling something was up but didn't say anything.

When we arrived at the cabins, he asked if we could take Georgia, our new dog, for a walk in the meadow.

Georgia was a Pomeranian-Corgi mix that we rescued in February 2018 as a Valentine's Day gift to each other. After over six months without a dog in the house, Matt and I were both ready to welcome a furry friend to our home. Our only requirement when we were looking was that we rescued the dog. Ideally, we wanted to bring in a middle-sized younger dog who liked to play, but those were bonuses. During our search, we visited the Oregon Humane Society multiple times and searched dozens of online rescue sites. When we saw Georgia's face, we knew we wanted to meet her.

"It says here that she's a thirty-five-pound Pomeranian-mix who loves to have fun," I read aloud to Matt. "She was found abandoned on the streets of Los Angeles." I pouted. "That's so sad."

Matt walked over to look at the single photo of the golden-hued dog with big round eyes that were lined with natural eyeliner.

"J-o-r-j-a," he read. "I've never seen it spelled that way."

"We could change the spelling," I joked. "We could tell people it's Georgia, like the state. Should I make an appointment to meet her?"

"Yeah, let's do it."

Before we could meet her, we had to talk to the owner of the rescue on the phone and do a home inspection, ensuring our environment was a safe place to welcome Georgia. The entire time, we worried that someone would rescue Georgia before we could meet her.

On a rainy Saturday afternoon, we made the ninety-minute-long drive to a dog park halfway between our house and the foster parents'. When we arrived, we saw Georgia on the leash.

"She's definitely not thirty-five pounds," I whispered to Matt.

"Not at all," he agreed. She was so much smaller than the website made her look.

With this being called a meet-and-greet, we thought we would meet Georgia and have time to decide if she would be a good fit. Instead, the foster parent sent us home with the dog, a leash, and the bag of food she was using.

"She's all yours," she told us.

"I guess we're dog owners again," Matt said. We both laughed and piled into the car, ready to start our new life as a family of three.

Georgia loved taking her sweet time on walks, sniffing every single flower, plant, or rock in her path. She'd be more than happy to explore the meadow behind the cabins.

"Sure," I replied. It was a beautiful day, blue skies peeking through the clouds.

When we finished walking the short loop, Matt asked if we could keep walking.

"Um, I guess..." I said, confused. We still hadn't gone into the room or unpacked our stuff.

We came upon two Adirondack chairs, and Matt asked if I wanted to sit.

"Why not," I said, sitting down in the chair on the right. Something was definitely up.

He asked me to play our favorite song, another weird thing that I went along with. Finally, he got up and stood over my left shoulder. He kneeled on one knee and went on to explain how much he loved me and how he wanted to spend our lives together.

"Will you marry me?" he asked nervously.

"Of course," I replied without hesitation, jumping up to hug him and give him a kiss.

He pulled the ring out of the box, and although it didn't fit—he'd accidentally sized it according to a ring that fit my pinky finger—it was absolutely stunning.

"I got the diamond from your mom when we were in Carmel," he told me. "She told me it was from the 1930s, which means this diamond probably belonged to your great-great grandmother."

"Wow!" I said in awe. I didn't have any family heirlooms, and this instantly became even more special than a standard engagement ring. "Thank you. I can't wait to marry you."

"I can't wait to marry *you*," he replied.

"So what do we do now?" I asked, laughing. It felt weird. "Call our families?"

"That's a good idea," I answered. "Mine or yours."

"Yours."

We meandered until we found a slim path that led to a secret hammock. We climbed into the hammock together and pulled Georgia on our laps. When the three of us were somewhat comfortable, I dialed my mom's number.

"Hi, daughter," she answered immediately.

"Hi, Mom. Is Dad with you?" I couldn't miss sharing this announcement with him.

"Lauren Shaber," he said, his voice booming across the room.

"Hi, Dad." I laughed. He always called me by my first and last name over the phone.

"Matt's here," I said. "We have some news. Let me put you on speaker."

"Hi, Matt!" My parents yelled in unison. They loved him as much as I did.

"We're getting married," I chimed in, unable to wait any longer.

"Congratulations!" My mom said, acting like she hadn't known this was coming.

"We're so happy for you two," my dad added.

"Tell us about the proposal!" My mom insisted.

We talked for a while, giving them the play-by-play of what happened and discussing potential wedding dates and locations. When Matt and I had exhausted every detail, my dad chimed in, "Beat it, kid. Go call Matt's parents and tell them the good news."

"Will do," I told him.

"Who loves you?" My dad ended every single call with the same question.

"You," I responded as I always did.

"How long for?"

"Always."

Regardless of if we were in person or on the phone, my dad and I finished every conversation with those same eight words. They never got old.

13

DISCOVERING THERAPY (IN MORE WAYS THAN ONE)

"You seriously need some girlfriends," my now-fiancé told me, yet again.

After two years in Oregon, the area was starting to feel like home. We had lived in a transitional apartment for a year before moving into a townhouse where we saw ourselves living for years to come. Everything we needed was within a five-mile radius, and we were closer to Matt's job so he no longer had to commute forty-five minutes each way. We lived along a beautiful trail that I walked along each morning before settling in for a day of remote work. While I loved the added productivity of working from home, I hated that I often went weeks without talking to anyone other than Matt or a grocery store clerk.

Each afternoon when he arrived home from work, I'd pounce, smothering Matt with questions: "Hi, love. How was your day? Want to go for a walk? Or maybe we could get dinner? What are you feeling? Maybe pho? Or should we just go casual with Chipotle? I can be ready in a few minutes if you want to go now." I didn't even give him a chance to say hi, much less breathe.

More often than not, all he wanted to do was sit on the couch and decompress for a few minutes. Mat was an introvert through and through, so being around people in an office all day was exhausting for him. Being closer to the office, he often walked or rode his bike to work and wanted to rest when he got home, especially on a rare sunny day. Even so, I itched to get out of the house after hours of being cooped up in my home office and begged for his company.

"How about a book club?" He had been encouraging me to meet local women, but I hadn't had the courage to put myself out there. As an extroverted introvert, I loved being with people but preferred to be in small groups and in places that I knew and recognized. I wasn't sure how to go about finding a friend group in Portland other than meeting people online, a prospect I wasn't super thrilled about.

"*Fine*." I sighed, giving in after his fifth suggestion. "I'll look into it."

One of my college roommates told me about a site called Meetup that she used to meet people upon moving to San Diego, so I figured I'd start there.

Maybe I could drop into an event and see what comes of it, I told myself. *I have nothing to lose.*

"Book club," I typed into the search bar, narrowing it down to events in Portland, Oregon.

At the top of the page was a meetup for something called the Girly Book Club. Their about page said the group was perfect for those who were new to Portland or who just wanted to discuss great books with like-minded friends. That was me, all right.

Turns out, it was a global book club with over one hundred thousand members across twelve countries; every member around the world read the same book over the same time period and then met up in their respective cities at the end of the month to discuss the book. I loved reading—I often read anywhere from fifty to one hundred books per year—and figured the worst that could happen was that I'd waste two hours of my time at the event and read a book I hated. On the plus side, at least I'd get a new book out of it.

July's event was a gathering at a wine bar in Southeast Portland. The group would be discussing *The Unseen World*, a novel by Liz Moore that I had never heard of. I clicked "Attend" before opening a new tab, going straight to Amazon to order the book. As I read the description, I grimaced. The science fiction-meets-mystery plot was definitely out of my comfort zone. I'd never pick this book off the shelf if I passed it in a bookstore.

You're going out of your comfort zone, I reminded myself before hitting "Add to cart." This was happening.

The book club became a constant on my calendar. Each month, I'd buy the book, often something I'd never think to pick up on my own, and show up ready to discuss. It gave me something to look forward to on the last Wednesday of the month. Even better, I connected with a woman who lived just down the street, and we got together on a regular basis for coffee, walks, and various outings throughout the week. For the first time since we moved to Oregon, I felt like I had a real friend.

At January 2018's meetup, the group of seven attendees decided to break out of the book club's rhythm and get together a few weeks later for an Olympic viewing party to celebrate the PyeongChang 2018 Olympic Winter Games. Despite being an athlete, I had never watched the opening ceremony before, and I looked forward to our rogue gathering. That day, the group became more than a book club; we became friends. Over the next few months, our friendship blossomed, growing into regular outings—hikes, brunch, Fourth of July parties, and birthdays—in addition to the book club. We became a close-knit group, listening to one another's struggles and supporting each other through the ups and the downs of jobs, relationships, and everyday life.

After enjoying an al fresco happy hour on a warm August afternoon with a few of the girls, I drove one of them home. As I parked in front of her complex, she asked a simple question: "How's work going?"

"You know what?" I responded. "It's not great."

I confessed that although I was up for a promotion, I felt trapped in my new role, and I was torn between pursuing consulting full-time or settling for corporate. By that point, I had shut down my blog but still felt pressure to create an online brand and presence, so I spent hours upon hours envisioning what that would look like. On top of everything, we were knee-deep in wedding planning, inadvertently creating an extravagant weekend affair that, for most, us included, would be a destination wedding. I broke down in tears as I relayed how overwhelmed I was.

For nearly forty-five minutes, she listened while I cried about the frustrations with my new job, my body, my relationship... everything. When I caught my breath, she told me gently that it might be worth reaching out to a professional counselor for support. She, like a couple of my other friends, was in therapy and had a good experience.

"I'm saying this because I care about you," she added, placing her hand on my shoulder.

"I'll think about it," I promised.

As a self-proclaimed workaholic, I convinced myself work was at the core of the burnout I was experiencing, so I started by exploring my company's employee assistance program. I learned we had access to three free sessions with a licensed counselor to discuss work stress. I booked an appointment with one of the first people who showed up on the directory of approved professionals and walked into her office a week later.

In our first session, we spent most of the time doing introductions before she slid her chair to the far corner of the room, leaving me sitting alone in the middle of her couch facing a blank white wall. She asked me to stare at the wall in front of me and, after a few minutes, told me to gaze at a different spot on the wall. We continued this way for twenty minutes, changing where I looked every minute or so, before she told me that our time was up. I had never heard of this kind of therapy technique before and wasn't experiencing any benefits other than confusion and frustration. I gave it three sessions before I quit.

Disappointed at using my free sessions to stare at a wall, I typed psychologytoday.com into my browser. My friend who urged me to try therapy recommended it when I told her how overwhelmed I was with the process of finding a counselor. In just a few clicks, I had a list of local counselors who focused on stress and were in my insurance network. I opened each profile in a different tab and narrowed it down until I had one person left. His bio talked about healing, transformation, and getting to a place where you feel "unstuck"—all things I desperately wanted and needed.

I clicked the "Email Me" button at the top of the page to send a request through the site. I hesitated, unsure of how to describe the level of discomfort I was feeling. I landed on short and sweet message:

> *Hi there, I feel like I am holding on to a lot of things emotionally, physically, and mentally, and am looking for someone to help me sort through them and let go. Do you offer a free consultation where we can see if this is a good fit? Looking forward to hearing from you.*

The next morning, he sent a kind reply back mentioning that, unfortunately, he doesn't offer consultations and confirmed that the therapeutic relationship needs to be a good fit for it to work. He did, however, seem open to chatting via email as a starting point, which I took him up on:

> *It's hard to put it into words, but I'll do my best.*

> *I wouldn't classify it as trauma, but I definitely feel like I'm holding on to a lot of things from my past (relationships, expectations, etc.) and constantly compare myself to my old self and others' expectations (or what I assume they expect of me). I'm also extremely overwhelmed and push myself to the breaking point*

seemingly every day. A few months ago, I went through a phase where I was so stressed that I was only getting three to four hours of sleep per night for six weeks straight, and I'm still dealing with the aftermath of that. I also have chronic jaw tension and neck tension, which my doctor thinks could be stemming from stress.

I have a lot of change and big life events happening right now: I'm getting married next month, am up for a promotion at my current role while also interviewing at other places, and am balancing consulting work. On top of that, my fiancé just got laid off. I also realize I could benefit from living a healthier lifestyle for various reasons, but I'm having an extremely difficult time committing to anything. I just don't have the energy or the motivation to commit to anything right now, especially myself. All of this is really taking a toll on my body, mental state, energy, sleep—everything. I'm sick of feeling exhausted and weighted down all the time.

Long story short, I want someone to talk through all of this with and help me figure out what my personal priorities are and how I can put some boundaries around them, for my own health and sanity. Is this something you can help with?

His friendly reply the next morning sold me. He told me that he knew the feeling and acknowledged how much I had going on. He told me I had good insight and getting some time to at least process it all would be very helpful. He said he could definitely help, and if I didn't think it was a good fit, he could assist in my search to find a therapist who was a better fit for me. I took a deep sigh and smiled as I replied back, coordinating our first appointment a few weeks later. He seemed like a real human being I could connect with on a personal level.

As soon as his appointment confirmation came through, my heart dropped. In his follow-up, he linked to his new patient forms and included a reminder that he isn't in-network for my insurance and that his cost was $150 per session, though he was open to negotiation if this price was too high.

I almost choked. $150 per hour? I thought he was covered by insurance. I went back in my browser history and, as it turned out, I forgot to filter out my insurance company. He was out of network. *Well, shit.*

I had a decision to make. I could go through the motions of finding another therapist or test the waters with him and see if I could bring his price down a bit. After reading and re-reading my email for the umpteenth time, proud of my honesty yet scared I said too much to a perfect stranger, I decided I couldn't wait. I booked his next appointment, which was a month out.

14

I DO

Fortunately, I didn't have to distract myself while waiting for the appointment. I had a wedding to plan and enjoy.

Matt and I decided to have a brunch wedding in Hood River, Oregon, just thirty minutes from the cabins where we got engaged. Over the years, we had visited Hood River a handful of times and fell in love with its small-town charm. The single main street reminded me of Carmel, and I couldn't wait to introduce our families to one of our favorite places in Oregon.

We were extremely fortunate when we came to coordinating the logistics. I found a wedding planner online and reached out asking if she'd be available for day-of services. In her email confirming that she was available and interested in working with us, she asked if we had a location in mind already. *If not,* she wrote, *I recommend looking at this new orchard. It should be built by the time September rolls around.*

I called the phone number she gave me and introduced myself to a kind woman on the phone. She said she was one of two owners of an up-and-coming wedding space. It would open the next year, and they'd be happy to give us a tour of the grounds. A few weeks later, Matt and I drove ninety minutes each way to tour what we envisioned would be a beautiful orchard. When we arrived, we were surprised to see a big dirt lot. If you looked south, you had a striking view of Mount Hood.

"It's not much," one of the owners said to us, "but we have a vision."

She went on to point out how the venue would be set up, where the ceremony would take place, and their contingency for unplanned rain during an event. She even explained what flowers they'd plant and where.

"I'm a florist," she told us, smiling. "I can't help it."

"Do you do weddings?" I asked, hoping she could do the flowers for our wedding, whether or not we chose to book with their venue.

"Because I'm so busy opening this space, I'm only going to do flowers for couples getting married at the orchard next year." I was sold.

Most of the other places I saw online did evening weddings, but I was the type of person who was in bed by ten every night.

"Is there any chance you'd be able to do a brunch wedding?" I asked.

"We were going to have all weddings start at 4:00 p.m., but we can make an exception for you," she said on the spot.

She told us that we'd be the first couple to book and would therefore receive a discount. We'd also have an opportunity to give feedback on things like chairs, tables, and linens as they ordered them for the event space. I loved the idea of being a local business' first customer, helping bring their vision to life. We had toured two other venues in Hood River, but Matt and I knew instantly that this was the one.

The owners of the orchard referred us to a caterer, who referred us to a DJ, who referred us to an officiant. The day-of coordinator recommended a makeup artist, hair stylist, gluten-free baker, and photographer. Because Hood River was a tight-knit community, all we had to do was find one person to start the domino effect. Our wedding came together seamlessly.

I became our unofficial wedding planner, keeping track of all wedding-related items in a spreadsheet that Matt and I both had access to. I kept a detailed to-do list with everything from "Finalize Georgia's plans for wedding week" to "Wedding favors" to "Create wedding website" and "Book honeymoon." I also kept a line-by-line breakdown of our budget. Between a welcome happy hour for all attendees, rehearsal dinner, and the wedding, I had my hands full in the month leading up to the wedding.

On top of coordinating the logistics, I created a wedding website and chose to design and print all of the signage, menus, and gift tags myself. I loved the creative process and dove head-first into figuring out which fonts, colors, and layout to use for each sign. My favorite was the menu we set on each plate that detailed the locally-sourced, farm-to-table dishes we served family style. In addition, I created a crossword puzzle that asked "How well do you know us?" giving attendees something to do while they waited for our families to take formal photos.

5-across: where we went on our first date
13-across: Matt's go-to coffee drink
3-down: day Lauren was born
17-down: our favorite hike in Oregon

Our wedding week was an absolute dream. Matt and I drove to Hood River on Tuesday, my parents arrived on

Wednesday, and his on Thursday. That night, we did a joint birthday to celebrate the three September birthdays in our immediate family; on Friday, we held the rehearsal dinner for our small wedding party; on Saturday, we hosted a welcome happy hour for all guests to stop by as they checked in; and on Sunday, September 15, just two days after my twenty-eighth birthday, we got married.

We had a small wedding, just sixty-five people, many of whom were visiting Oregon for the first time. Our goal was to try and make them fall in love with the state, just as we had. As part of our first look before the ceremony, we read our own vows under the rain; during the ceremony, we read a different version. We each had our oldest friend by our side during the ceremony. My brother, the most outgoing person I know—my parents always joked he could make a friend with a camel in a desert—took the reception to another level. While Matt and I were taking photos, he challenged everyone to fill out the crossword puzzle. Anyone who filled in the entire thing would be entered to win a bottle of wine and a pear plucked from the orchard, both signed by me and Matt.

"And the winner is..." he announced into the microphone.

He burst out laughing before he could explain what was so funny. He looked around the room seriously. "Where's Mr. J?" he asked.

Our relative put their head down in shame. "You're disqualified! You left every item blank."

The entire room started laughing together. I picked a second folded piece of paper from the jar, which was accurately filled in.

"The real winner is a member from the Book Club Babes!" My brother always got my book club confused with the short-lived joint blog I had with my fitness friends a few years prior. I couldn't help but smile.

Over the next two hours, Matt and I continued to have one of the most special days of our lives. We purposefully planned it so we could not only be present with our guests, but enjoy the food, cake, and music. It was the first time our families and closest friends had ever been in the same room—much less, the same state—together, and we wanted to soak it up.

Just before we gathered for cake, one of Matt's cousins gave us the biggest surprise either of us ever could have expected.

"Matt! Lauren!" she called us over. "We have a surprise for you."

She led the two of us to the grass, away from the crowd, and handed Matt a phone. We both looked at her in confusion.

"Okay, Grandpa, they're here!"

"Congratulations," we heard through the phone.

Tears streamed down both of our eyes as we saw Matt's grandfather show up on the little phone screen. I'd met Matt's grandfather once over the years, and he became the grandfather I never had growing up. The first time we met, I was sitting in a comfy leather chair in his condo skimming through one of his cookbooks while we waited for him to come out. When he came out of his room, he rolled his wheelchair straight to where I was sitting.

"Ah, Bobby Flay," he said, eyeing the book I was flipping through. "One of my favorites."

"One of mine, too," I said, smiling back at him.

"I haven't seen this cookbook before, though" I added. "Bobby looks really young in the photo on the cover." I turned it toward him so he could see. "I wonder when it was published?" I flipped to the copyright information. Turns out, it was Bobby's first book, published in May 1994.

I closed the book, adding it back to the pile under the side table, and tuned into the conversation. Matt's side of the family was trickling in to celebrate Thanksgiving together, and it was the first time I was meeting most of his extended family.

After we returned to the hotel that afternoon, someone dropped off a thick package with my name written in shaky handwriting on the cover. When I opened the flap, I was stunned. It was *Bobby Flay's Bold American Food.* I read the accompanying note as tears started pooling in my eyes. *I wanted you to have this,* it started. The note finished with, *I'm so glad you're part of our family.*

Me too, Grandpa B, me too.

Seeing Matt's grandpa on his cousin's phone at the wedding took me right back to that moment. I started bawling uncontrollably as a myriad of emotions washed over me. I was so happy to see him, grateful to his family for making this happen with the limited cell service, and overwhelmed by the feeling of love surrounding me and Matt. We were in our favorite place, surrounded by our favorite people. Nothing could top that feeling.

Leave it to my brother to find a way to elevate the day even further. For our last dance, we asked the DJ— who also played live acoustic guitar—to sing a version of "Falling Slowly," a song Matt had played for me on the guitar early on in our relationship. He announced that the last dance was starting and asked all attendees to gather in a circle around us. My cheeks burned in embarrassment for approximately one second before I got lost in the music, looking at Matt.

A minute or so in, we saw bubbles floating over our heads, and before we knew it, everyone in the circle had taken the bubbles we set aside for our exit and started blowing them into the circle. I can't say for sure that my brother instigated this, but I have a gut feeling he did. Whoever did, thank you. It was the most magical moment.

Instead of setting off on our European honeymoon right after the wedding, we opted to do what we called a minimoon, a shorter local trip, giving ourselves time to breathe after such a hectic week. We spent the first two nights back at our favorite cabins, before making our way three hours south to Bend for a night. On the fourth day, we drove to Crater Lake, which was hands-down one of the most beautiful places I had ever seen. The sapphire blue water rivaled that of Greece, and I couldn't help but fall even more in love with Oregon. We were beyond fortunate to call this state home.

15

ANOTHER DIAGNOSIS, ANOTHER SLEEPLESS NIGHT

Just days after returning from our mini-moon, I stepped foot in the therapist's cramped office for the first time. The room was just big enough for a couch, a desk, and a few bookshelves, all of which were overflowing with books. Paperback books were *everywhere*. Every ounce of space was covered, making me feel even more overwhelmed than when I walked in.

"So tell me why you're here," he asked.

I rattled off exactly what I said in the email—that I was feeling overwhelmed and exhausted.

"Let's pick somewhere to start," he encouraged.

"Work," I responded without hesitation.

I was a self-proclaimed workaholic. The wedding was the first time I had taken off two consecutive weeks in my entire career, and it definitely wasn't an opportunity to rest and reset. I thought about work twenty-four-seven and never turned off. I told him the frustration I felt working under a micromanager, the disappointment that settled in when I realized I wasn't fairly compensated for the work I was doing, and the guilt I felt for looking for a new role after such a short amount of time. I also told him about the consulting business I had on the side, and how overwhelmed I felt trying to balance client work on top of working full time, wedding planning, and other life stressors.

"You also mentioned trauma in your email. What did you mean by that?" he asked.

"Oh, I think I just wrote it in the moment." I shrugged it off, turning the conversation back to work. Work was my safe place, my identity. It was easy to talk about what I do every day; talking about childhood trauma, on the other hand? It was too much to handle. Thankfully, our fifty minutes ended soon after.

I came back the following week to pick up where we left off. For ten weeks, I showed up at his door to talk about life; instead, I focused the conversation solely on my career. I never mentioned my two diagnoses and the cardiologist's voice telling me I wasn't crazy even though I felt phantom heartbeats. I didn't want to be judged, even by a professional. *Especially* by a professional.

After our tenth session, when I felt like we dragged the work conversation out long enough, I told him via email that I was ready for a break. I blamed it on the cost when, in reality, I was scared to dive deeper into other conversations. During those ten sessions, I felt good. I was proud of myself for going to and prioritizing therapy, but when I stepped away from it all, I fell right back into my old rhythm, feeling exhausted and burned out, holding the weight of the world on my shoulders with each step I took.

I continued to show up to work, book club, special events, and holiday gatherings, but behind my smile was pure and utter exhaustion. I was tired of going to doctor after doctor and getting insufficient answers. Despite having a loving husband at home who tried his absolute best to support me, I felt alone as I navigated life with not one, but two autoimmune diseases, grieving the life I once knew while trying to adjust to one with chronic illness. Matt didn't experience the pain, discomfort, and nausea I did all day, every day, and he could only do so much to do help relieve my pain. After getting laid off from my corporate job and watching my savings deplete, I felt like a complete failure, despite securing a new full-time job. I was still trapped underwater in the sea of negative comments on the gossip forum and Instagram, watching my online presence fade before my eyes. I was barely sleeping, and I looked and felt like a zombie. I wasn't sure how much longer I could hold on.

In an effort to find out who I was, I completely isolated myself, distancing from everyone I knew. I stopped texting and calling friends and family, curious who, if anyone, would reach out to me first. Each day, I asked myself difficult questions like, *Who am I?* and *What's my purpose?* leading to an even deeper feeling of isolation and loneliness when I couldn't answer. I felt totally and utterly lost.

"How's it going, love?" Matt would ask me.

"It's fine," I'd reply, monotone.

"Are you sure you're okay?"

"Yeah, I'm fine."

"Okay," he replied, "I'm here if you need me. I love you."

Even to my husband, I turned sour and emotionless. When we watched TV at night, I'd settle in on the opposite side of the couch, as far as physically possible. I'd spend the hour absorbed in my phone, playing games or doom-scrolling instead of cuddling with him like I normally would. I couldn't tell Matt what was going on. I was afraid that if I did, I would scare him away. That the "always on" girl he fell in love with was really just broken and messed up.

To compensate, I emotionally distanced myself as much as I could while living in the same house. My typically long and animated answers to, "How was your day, love?" became, "Fine. Yours?" The same response made my skin crawl when Matt or colleagues said it to me. Despite pushing him away, Matt checked in on a daily, sometimes hourly basis, reminding me that he loved me. That he was there. Still, nothing changed.

Six months later, the COVID-19 pandemic hit.

Because I was already in self-isolation, adjusting to quarantine wasn't difficult. It made things easier, to be honest. I didn't have to give excuses for why I didn't want to meet with friends anymore; going out wasn't even an option. For months, I continued doing what I was doing: distancing myself from everyone but colleagues and burning the candle at both ends.

Work was my solace, the easiest place for me to put on a mask. I would throw on a sweatshirt over my pajamas, plaster on a smile, and talk in a higher pitch than I normally would. As part of the communications team, I was responsible for writing communications on behalf of senior leaders, telling their teams to, "Take care of yourselves during this unprecedented time." I never followed my own advice.

Instead of delivering 150 percent at work, I gave ninety, the max I could muster. I would wear the same sweatshirt for days on end, not caring if the person on the other side of the screen noticed. I went days without brushing my teeth and weeks without washing my hair, two tasks I performed on a daily basis. It was all I could do to show up and complete my work on time; taking care of myself fell to the back burner.

I reminded myself every day how fortunate I was. I had a roof over my head; a husband and dog who loved me; a job that paid the bills and more; the most supportive parents who visited regularly and answered every call without hesitation; close friends. I struggled to see the good through the darkness of my trauma that was bubbling up to the surface.

In my annual check-up with my primary care doctor that summer, in addition to discussing weight gain, I finally opened up about the funk I had been living in for the past four years. I hesitantly told her about the darkness that loomed above my head ever since I started receiving and reading negative comments about laurenliveshealthy all those years ago, quietly berating myself for letting the internet affect me so badly.

At the end of my long-winded monologue, she encouraged me to address the depression and anxiety instead of focusing on weight loss.

"We have a couple of options," she said. "You can try therapy and other home remedies like meditation, or you can go on an antidepressant."

"I've already tried therapy, and it hasn't helped as much as I would have liked," I said cautiously.

"It's also pretty expensive," I added as I mentally calculated the six hundred dollars per month I'd have to spend if I went back to my therapist at full price.

"In that case, I recommend we try the medication."

"Can I sleep on it and let you know tomorrow?" I was hesitant to commit to another lifelong drug.

"No problem," she replied. "I'll put in the order in case you decide to start the medication. Just let me know what you decide to do and we'll go from there."

My mind ping-ponged as I drove to the pharmacy to pick up the prescription, opting to pick it up on my way home so I didn't have to venture out the next day.

"Your total is $1.92," the pharmacist told me.

Well, that's a lot cheaper than therapy, I mused.

Even though this appointment led to a massive fight with my insurance company—it went from a free annual check-up to a three-hundred-dollar mental health appointment, which, according to my insurance company, I, the patient, should have prevented—it was well worth my time. I felt a weight lift off my chest when I said the words, "I'm in a funk" out loud and started to believe this medicine could help. I took the first pill an hour later.

We were well into the pandemic by this point, so I'm sure I wasn't the first to show up on my doctor's doorstep struggling with mental health challenges, but I still felt alone as I faced my additional diagnoses of generalized anxiety disorder and clinical depression. I only knew one person in real life who took anxiety medication, and it was for weight loss purposes, not anxiety.

After taking the medication for a few weeks, I woke up one morning in a complete panic, my heart racing, like a hummingbird was stuck inside of my chest.

What the hell? I asked myself as I shot up to a sitting position.

When I picked up the antidepressant, the pharmacist warned me that I might experience vivid dreams, but they didn't tell me I'd dream about my ex-boyfriend every freaking night. The dreams had been happening for thirty days straight. I knew because the first one happened the night I started taking the medication. I hadn't gone one night without seeing my ex's face. I wasn't sure I believed in God, but I started to pray to something—anything—to make the dreams stop.

Because they were hyper-realistic, the dreams were a special form of torture. When my ex died in my arms, I woke up feeling the physical weight of holding someone's life in my hands. When we were in bed together, I woke up confused, wondering why my husband was sleeping next to me instead of my ex. When we were walking the dog, I saw Gigi's small frame walking next to me on the leash, not Georgia's.

Each interaction felt so real, like I was living out a parallel life that would have happened had my ex and I not broken up eight years prior. When I woke up, it took me a few seconds to realize I was at home, in Oregon, in 2020.

"I need to change my medication," I told my doctor at our six-month check-in.

Other than the dreams, the medication seemed to be working. According to my assessments, my anxiety and depression levels had both leveled out, down significantly from when I first went on the pill eight months earlier. Even so, I was desperate to avoid the vivid dreams. They messed with my head too much.

"I'm putting you on a similar medication," my doctor said. "If it doesn't work for any reason, we can easily switch back. No problem."

"What about the phentermine?" I asked. "Will it be too much to start two new medications at once?"

The week before, I had finally, after an eighteen-month wait, seen a second endocrinologist that focused on weight management. Although I was otherwise healthy and able to swim miles on end, my doctors were all concerned about my weight, and my endocrinologist referred me to an even more specialized colleague. Based on BMI, I was obese and felt every extra pound hanging from my body. My knees hurt, I was winded walking up a single flight of stairs, and I genuinely hated the way I looked. When my endocrinologist referred me to this even more specialized specialist, I was more than open to it. Losing weight is more difficult for people with thyroid issues, and I could take all the expertise and support I could get.

"We need to look at two key hormones," the specialist told me via Zoom.

"Ghrelin is your hunger hormone, which is released when your stomach is empty and tells you when it's time to eat," he explained. "Leptin, on the other hand, is the hormone released by your fat cells to tell your brain when you've had enough to eat."

I very rarely, if ever, felt full, so I wasn't surprised when he told me that my body released high levels of ghrelin, making me think I was hungry all the time, even when I wasn't. His specialty, he told me, was prescribing a series of medications to trick my body into thinking satiety hormones were being released.

"We'll start with a medication called phentermine," he said. "It's a stimulant designed to decrease appetite. Take half a dose for the first few weeks and move up to the full dose when you feel you've adjusted to the medication. When your weight loss plateaus in six to nine months, we'll start a second medication. Any questions?"

I had a lot of questions but had a hard time formulating the words, instead promising to contact him if any concerns came up. After I disconnected from the virtual meeting, I called my dad. He was aware of every doctor's appointment I had gone to and had been looking forward to this appointment as much as I had.

"What are your thoughts on phentermine?" I asked as soon as he answered.

"It's been around for sixty years," he said. "It's used and trusted by a lot of doctors."

By the end of our call, I decided to try it. We both agreed to trust the experts. Plus, the doctor promised his team would be available for support along the way. What could go wrong?

Four weeks later, as both the phentermine and the new antidepressant kicked in, my body went into overdrive.

Instead of my normal eight to nine hours of sleep per night, I was getting three to four. Like clockwork, I woke up starving at 3:00 a.m., even though I went to bed on a full stomach. I was also extremely jittery and on edge throughout the day, like I had consumed three shots of espresso, despite drinking just one shot of decaf each morning. According to my Fitbit, my resting heart rate had gone from forty-eight beats per minute to sixty-eight beats per minute in a matter of weeks, averaging well over a hundred each day instead of my normal sixty.

I explained all of this in separate messages to my primary care doctor and the weight loss endocrinologist, asking if it could be a drug interaction between the phentermine and the new antidepressant.

It was unlikely, both the specialist's nurse and my primary care doctor explained.

On the phone with a nurse from the specialist's office, she urged me to stay on the phentermine, promising that was the only way I'd lose weight.

"What about the sleep?" I asked in response.

"We can prescribe a third medication to address that," the nurse responded. "It's what the doctor would recommend."

"I'll think about it," I responded. I wasn't happy on the medication, and neither was my body, but I didn't want to make a rash decision in the moment.

"Send us a message letting us know what you decide," she said, ending the call.

For days, I agonized over my response, my mind writing and rewriting the email I would send. Although I had lost nearly twenty pounds and felt good physically, I was sleep-deprived, moody, and experiencing suicidal thoughts on a regular basis. My moods were affecting everything from work to my marriage, and I was in desperate need of a good night's sleep. I needed sleeping pills, not a medication to address the side effect of another medication.

You know your body better than anyone else, I told myself. *Follow your instinct.* My gut was telling me that the phentermine, not the antidepressants, were causing the negative symptoms.

For the first time in my life, I stood up for myself to a doctor: *I'm not sure staying on the medication is the best course of action for my body,* I wrote in an email to the nurse. *I'd love to explore other options.*

This is the course of action we prescribe for all of their patients, she replied a few hours later. *There are no other options.*

When I saw her email, my jaw immediately tightened. I waited eighteen months for an appointment with a specialist, just to get a one-size-fits-all treatment? I let the anger wear off before I responded.

> *I am willing to do whatever it takes to get some sleep. I've been tracking it, and the last time I got a full night's sleep was on April 2, so it's been almost six weeks. The insomnia is now getting in the way of daily life and isn't sustainable for much longer. Please let me know what you would recommend as an immediate solution.*

Thanks for your message, her reply started. *I would suggest stopping the medication now—sleep disruptions can add up so I suggest getting back to a regular sleep cycle. I will ask the doctor what else he suggests for medical weight loss. Please let me know if you have further questions or concerns.*

She never followed up.

I stopped the phentermine immediately, but that didn't stop a mental breakdown from happening.

16

IN LOVING MEMORY

On March 30, 2021, I did what I always do after work. I curled up on the couch with my computer on my lap, ready to zone out. That evening, I went to Instagram to check in on the people I followed for so many years; those I felt like I knew as friends, even though we had never met.

I started by catching up on the feed of one of my old-time favorites whose photos I had missed over the last few months. Instead of looking through photos of her cute kids and healthy recipes, I got caught on her most recent post. The caption started with "[Trigger warning]" and went on to explain how a fellow creative took her own life a few days before. One line in particular stood out: "yoga, green juice and a lot of followers can't bring you joy—it only comes from within."

I instantly felt dizzy and my hands clammed up, making the keyboard slip under my grip. A vivid memory from a few years prior popped into my mind. I hadn't posted in a few hours and wanted to make an Instagram story showing my green smoothie routine. I couldn't show my face in the post because I was crying, feeling like my perfect-on-paper life wasn't enough for me; instead,

I showed the blender whirring as it mixed the orange, banana, and spinach together. My stomach clenched as the memory settled into my body. I saw myself so deeply in this post and needed to know more about the girl featured in the accompanying video.

I was an avid follower of an LA-based health influencer with the same first name, so I instantly opened a new tab and brought up her profile. She'd posted a few minutes prior, so I knew she hadn't died. Relief washed over me— until curiosity took over. The post hadn't mentioned the woman's Instagram handle, much less her last name, so I started googling. Within moments, I found her profile and was exploring the feed of someone who seemingly had the dream life. A slight smile crossed my face as I scrolled through her photos. She appeared to be happily in love, having recently announced a new relationship after a very public breakup. The deeper I went into her archives, the more I learned. For the past few years, she had been traveling the world with her ex-boyfriend, documenting their travels in a converted sprinter van on a shared YouTube channel. After the split, she started her own channel, bought her own van and was already documenting the entire process of building it into a home on wheels. From her photos, you'd think she had it all.

My heart simultaneously broke and expanded as I clicked from photo to photo, reading each caption in depth. They weren't just talking about the good things in life like everything was perfect; in her most recent posts, she talked about her anxiety and how she was feeling off balance. She showed the "real" side of taking an Instagram photo by explaining that although the photo looked nice, she was actually covering up a cold sore caused by stress. She shared how difficult it can be to open up and share things with the public and didn't apologize for being herself. She also talked about things like goals and dreaming big and making deeper connections.

During my scrolling frenzy, I came across a video, posted by her on December 5, 2020. Within the first minute, a young blonde showed up on screen, holding a white mug with a heart made from two halves of an avocado on it—a near-replica of the image on my favorite t-shirt—talking about how, despite living a life that looked perfect to the external world, she was struggling.

"What I've learned with depression and anxiety," she says while looking up, away from the camera, "is that depression is being stuck in the past and anxiety is being stuck in the future, and, ultimately, when you're feeling this way, you're not able to truly be present in the moment."

Four minutes and thirty seconds into the video, I watched her open her computer and navigate to her Notes app to read her "brain dump" from July 2020 aloud:

I feel unable to take care of myself. Basic needs like feeding myself are hard right now. I feel lazy and disgusted with myself for how little I'm able to take care of. I'm unable to focus on anything, really. I feel like I should be doing work. I should be making a LinkedIn profile. I feel sad, lost, and lonely. I'm unable to focus. I'm constantly comparing myself. I feel like I need to be productive meanwhile I'm spending my whole day procrastinating. Now I feel worse that I haven't accomplished anything. I did go for a bike

ride with Dad today. That was nice. I just woke up
on the wrong side of the bed. I do truly want to create
a morning routine to look forward to. I want to wake
up each day excited to live that day. Right now, living
feels like a drag. I have a hard time envisioning my
future because I don't know what I want, yet I'm not
focusing on figuring out what I want. I know what I
don't want and that list is long... so how can I be so
picky? I always think a new place will solve my issue;
new surroundings, new friends, but it's not that simple.
I'm working on becoming better at being me—who I am,
where I am—but it's hard. This is a mental battle that
I'm losing miserably right now. I am not appreciating
what I have or what's around me. I speak the words
but I don't feel it.

When she finished reading the passage, I paused the video to catch my breath. My eyes started to water as I realized how similar our stories were. Like me, she seemed to want to get to know people on a deep level; to show life beyond the filters, curated feeds, and perfect captions. She seemed like someone I'd say hi to—or at least smile at—if we happened to be at the same event. I envisioned us getting coffee, diving deep into existential questions about the purpose and power of social media, and becoming close friends.

I had also written a version of this journal entry. Although it was just over a year prior, I remembered the moment vividly. I was sitting at the kitchen counter, the dishwasher running in the background, and a watered-down decaf iced latte next to my laptop. A rare urge to journal came over me, so I grabbed my computer and pulled up my Notes app. Unsure of where to start, I wrote about what happened that morning:

I weighed myself for the first time in a while this morning, I typed. *It wasn't just a glance, as I've done in passing over the last few years, it was a wake-up-call moment, and what I saw made me so sad, so disappointed in myself.*

Over the next half hour, I wrote lines upon lines of stream of consciousness, calling myself adjectives like pathetic and scolding myself for gaining weight, sharing my story online, and even joining the women's health program at all. I admitted to being in denial, pretending to the world that I was strong when, in reality, I felt anything but. As soon as my energy depleted, leaving me unable to write anymore, I read the entry back to myself. As I re-read the last line—*I've lost so much confidence in myself*—I sobbed, soaking the keyboard with tears.

Writing that note was the most honest I had ever been with anyone, especially myself. As I processed the negative undertones of my journal entry, I fell into a tug-of-war in my mind. My first instinct was that I was being dramatic, that I shouldn't write such depressing things because I have a beautiful life that I should be happy with and proud of. At the same time, I was applauding myself for being so open about my feelings. I was so used to hiding behind a smile that it felt freeing in a way to share my truth. Regardless of whether anyone saw it, writing this note was the first time I really gave myself permission to wholeheartedly feel my feelings.

After composing myself, both from hearing the woman's note in the video and recalling my own memory,

I pressed play to continue watching. Before long, I was bawling, crying along with her as she talked through tears about how she cut off her friendships and purposefully put herself in isolated situations so no one would know if she died.

"But I had a dog," she said through tears and sniffles. "And my dog looked me in my eyes, and I couldn't leave my dog."

I had to pause the video *again* to regroup. I had seen photos of her ex-boyfriend's dog on Instagram. The larger-than-life, white and gray Australian Shepherd had big round eyes and a large mouth that always seemed to be smiling. *I wouldn't be able to leave him either,* I thought.

Over the coming weeks, I got lost in her content, spending hours upon hours each day reading Instagram captions from years past, watching old YouTube videos, and even listening to a podcast she had recorded a few months prior with another van-life couple.

At ninety minutes, the podcast was longer than anything I had listened to in months, but I was eager to absorb more of her vivacious energy. In the interview, she talked to her close friends about her breakup, stopping van life, and her mental health journey, including the immense bullying she endured a couple months prior when she introduced her new boyfriend on the joint channel she shared with her ex-boyfriend.

I tried to listen as I cleaned the kitchen, but I had to sit down on the couch so I could focus. In the same way I wanted to lock eyes with a friend over dinner to let them know I was listening to every word, I wanted to give the podcast my undivided attention. Just over an hour in, I pressed pause; it felt too raw—too real—picturing a now-friend struggling so much. It would be a full week before I'd be able to press play and listen to the last thirty minutes. With each Instagram post, YouTube video, and podcast interview I read or listened to in the following weeks, I thought, *I could have written this verbatim.*

As I explored her pages and saw the outpouring of love and support in the wake of the tragic news about her, I learned that she had been a victim of serious cyberbullying in the months leading up to her death, more than she let on in the podcast interview. According to the Instagram post where I first learned about the tragedy, "the very last screenshot on [her] phone was a nasty long comment from a YouTube follower who thought she was 'helping' (???) [sic] by leaving hate."

"Congrats," the poster wrote, "you left such an impression that she took a screenshot of the comment."

Like this woman, I knew first-hand how much power a comment from a stranger could have, and it's devastating. For many years, I was so caught up in my own story, feeling like I had to carry the burden of shame and regret all by myself, that I honestly didn't realize thousands of others out there had similar pain and experiences.

Ironically, I found solace in the comment section, which is very rare in the online world. One video, in particular—a tribute video posted by her two best friends, the couple who hosted the podcast interview—helped me feel part of a community that I never knew I needed, much less existed. In the comment section, people around the world shared their own stories of in-person and online bullying and how it led to irrational thoughts, depression and, in some cases, attempted suicide. They shared that, because of the woman's story, they were getting help by going to therapy, trying meditation, writing, reaching out to loved ones—all the tools the woman had advocated for and encouraged. They said they felt seen and were grieving her loss, just like I was.

People were commenting that, although they never knew her in real life, they were deeply affected, some even unable to watch the full video. A few commenters shared their own suicidal stories while others reflected on the pain and guilt of losing a loved one to mental illness. Intertwined with these were hundreds, maybe even thousands, of comments encouraging fellow readers and grievers to reach out to loved ones for support. Feeling inspired, I did just that.

17

WRITING TO HEAL

For the next hour, as I alternated between pacing back and forth in my bedroom and lying supine on the carpet at the foot of our bed, I opened up to my family in ways I never had before.

Mental health wasn't really a thing in our family. We talked about our days over dinner, but it was surface level. Growing up, I didn't know anyone who went to therapy, and I saw meditation as a woo-woo practice. I considered downward dog, not to mention an entire yoga class, to be the opposite of relaxation, and I never considered journaling as a way to manage my emotions. It wasn't until I reached out to my mom before our Utah trip that I openly talked about my feelings with my immediate family. Anxiety and depression, much less mental health, weren't in my vocabulary until my late twenties.

Maybe it was my age or the people I surrounded myself with online and in person, or even society as a whole, but I often felt alone in my struggles. Part of me assumed others weren't okay, but I couldn't really grasp that thought because it never showed. Friends were always happy and smiling, venting about school, sports, and boys. They never mentioned depression or anxiety, my family even less so. When people go through hard times, they don't talk about how they wear the same clothes three days in a row or are unable to get out of bed; instead, they just don't talk about it. They simply pretend those moments don't exist. So I did, too. Until I read the comments on the tribute video of the influencer who took her own life.

They'll never know how much you're struggling unless you tell them, I reminded myself.

I started by texting my brother:

Me: Hey, do you remember [the bully] from [middle school]?

My brother: [Name]?

Me: Yeah. I'm doing some reflecting and just started thinking about what he put me through. Do you remember how miserable he made me?

My brother: I don't remember. Do you want to share or talk about it? I believe you. He was a bully.

Me: Sure, we can talk about it. I didn't realize you didn't know. It's messed me up for years.

Due to misaligned timing, we resorted to a text conversation, which was out of character for us. My texts to my brother often went unread, so phone calls were our default form of communication.

Me: I was so mad at you and mom for years (you're obviously both forgiven now), but I'm realizing neither of you probably knew how bad it was. I don't think I've ever told anyone the details, even Matt. You'll be the first to know.

My brother: I'm ready to listen. I can't go back in time and be there for you, but I can be here for you now. And make you a lifetime, deep in my bones promise that I'll always be there for you and have your back.

My heart melted, tears welling in my eyes. My brother and I have had a wishy-washy relationship over the years. Some of my fondest memories involve my younger brother: him kneeling on the floor, petting bees, waiting to see if they'd sting him in return; hiding under the coffee table together, deathly afraid of the life-sized Barney that stood in our living room wishing us happy birthday; the two of us trying to rescue a mouse from our shared bathroom without screaming or waking our parents.

Unfortunately, those memories are also tainted with feelings of resentment, frustration, and sadness: when he didn't stand up for me in middle school, when he shared an inappropriate post about me on Facebook for all of our friends and classmates to see, when he started dating a close friend of mine in senior year of high school, thereby "stealing" her from me. It wasn't until we lived on two different continents well into our twenties that our relationship started evolving from a forced relationship into a true friendship. His promising to have my back only solidified our connection even more.

After realizing that my brother hadn't remembered the bullying despite being present for some of it, I was curious what, if anything, my mom recalled. She answered after the second ring.

"I have a random question for you," I said after our initial hellos and how are yous.

"Do you remember [that kid] from middle school?" I asked curiously.

"All I remember is that I found a message that he posted on your Myspace," she replied. "That was awful."

"I don't think I ever told you—or anyone—how bad it was." I went on to relay his four-times-per-day routine. "And then, when you found out, you went straight to the principal without even giving me a heads-up. And *then*," I laid it on her, "after you promised me you wouldn't, you told your sister what happened. I was mad at you for a long time."

"I had no idea," she replied. "I'm so sorry. For all of it. I wish I could have done better by you. I didn't know."

"It's okay." I sighed. "You were doing the best you could with the information you had. I forgave you a long time ago."

As we continued talking, she told me how surprised she was that I was still holding on so tightly to these memories. Knowing how writing, for me, is a form of therapy, she proposed that I write a letter to my middle school bully; whether I sent it to him or not didn't matter— maybe just writing it down would help.

"While we're going back in time, want to hear another funny story?" I asked, changing the subject.

"Of course," she replied, always willing to listen.

I told her about my friend who texted me instead of her boyfriend, commenting about my shirt. "To this day, I wish I had left them in Safeway," I said, ending my monologue.

"I'm so surprised," my mom said. "I thought she was your best friend!"

"Not after that," I scoffed. My mom didn't know what she and our other friends put me through in the random guy's apartment, and I wasn't about to tell her.

"Can you imagine their faces?" I asked, coming back to the text message discussion. I burst out in laughter as I tried to describe the shock they might have felt if I'd left them at Safeway. Within seconds, my abs hurt and my eyes watered.

"How funny would that have been if they walked out and realized I wasn't in the parking lot?" I asked. My laughter was contagious. I heard my mom laughing in the background, wheezing along with me.

When our laughter died down, my mom said, "Honestly? She would have deserved it." I knew an eye roll accompanied that, even though I couldn't see it.

"Yeah," I said quietly. "She would have. That was messed up."

For a split second, it felt like the clouds were parting and a rainbow was shining through. It was raw and emotional and beautiful to open up to my mom in such an honest way.

After disconnecting, I attempted to take my mom's advice. I started a note in my phone titled "A letter to my middle school bully" but struggled to figure out what to say. It took me three days to find the words.

I started by writing, *You probably don't remember me, but I remember you,* and went on to recall the horrible things he said to me.

Instead of being a welcome break in between classes, the lockers were my personal hell during the school day. While I was gathering my books for the next class, I also had to deal with you.

I summarized the comments he made before writing:

It wasn't just one time or one day. It was every break, every day, for two years. Let's break that down. Assuming you made four comments a day and we estimate there are 180 days in each school year, that's approximately 1,440 times that you drilled it into my brain that I was fat, bigger, different; a total of 360 days that I had to endure your cruelty.

I told him how his words didn't just go in one ear and out the other; they seeped into me and became ingrained in who I was.

Over time, I started seeing myself how you did: as a whale no one would ever love. You convinced me I was unworthy; a waste of space; a fat pig. I believed it down to my core, and I assumed everyone else saw me that way too.

I told him that, because of his comments, my life started revolving around weight loss and restriction, turning into a rollercoaster of strict dieting, binge eating, and body dysmorphia that would last for years—maybe even a lifetime. I also told him about some other instances that made me feel inferior: when I wanted to try out for cheerleading but convinced myself not to because I couldn't even fit in the uniform, when I lied about my weight on my driver's license, and the time my friends and I shopped at Forever21 for the first time.

I can still feel the shame I felt when I realized I was the only one who was limited to the plus-sized section in the furthest, darkest corner of the store, I wrote.

In addition, I explained how every aspect of my lifestyle changed in an effort to become who I thought he and others wanted me to be.

I started to think of my worth in terms of numbers: the number on the scale, the number of calories I ate, the size on the tag of my clothes. I lived a life of restriction, constantly undereating and overtraining, hell-bent on getting to a weight where I could be considered "normal" for just once in my life.

Until this week, I continued, *I didn't tell a soul, not even my mom, how much you put me through.*

No one knew how often you made fun of me and how much your words affected me, but they did; they do. Because of you, I always strived to be someone else. I wanted to be thinner and lighter and prettier so I'd be seen as worthwhile, not worthless. At times I felt like I couldn't handle the name-calling and tormenting, but

I persevered and made it through. Unfortunately, a lot of people can't.

I went on to tell him about the influencer who died by suicide and the cyber-bullying she experienced in the days, weeks, and months leading up to her death. I wrote, *I share this to show that bullying, in-person or online, can have extreme consequences.*

I ended the letter with the most honest words I had ever written:

If you read this, I hope you realize that your words weren't just words, especially to a young girl who didn't know any better and wasn't strong enough to stand up for herself. Your words were toxic and harmful and caused a domino effect of other emotions and challenges that I'll likely struggle with my entire life. I sincerely hope no one else has experienced the trauma you put me through.

It only took nineteen years, but I'm starting to realize I am worth it. I'm fortunate to have a strong support system filled with a husband, a brother, parents, and friends who love me and support me. I'm grateful to have access to healthcare and professionals who can help me work through and overcome the body dysmorphia and weight-related anxiety if it gets to be too much.

As I typed the final line, I sat straighter than I had in years.

I'm starting to realize that my size doesn't define me— and neither do you.

Last I heard, he lived in a different state—Missouri, maybe—and had a young child with a former fling. Tempted to send him a copy of the letter, I tracked down the address of his family's business. His parents were prominent members of the community and owned a number of businesses throughout Monterey County, so it wasn't hard to find their contact information. Within minutes, I had the address for their business headquarters.

Thinking I could send the letter to them with a note asking to forward it to their son, I printed out the typed document, sealed it in an envelope, and added postage. However, I never got the courage to send it; to this day, the letter is still in my car, addressed, licked, sealed, and stamped, ready to be dropped off at the post office.

Instead, I decided to publish the letter online, knowing from experience that sharing my words with strangers would make it—writing, reflecting, letting go—feel real. I had only one challenge—nowhere to post it. My blog was long gone, and I didn't want to create a new one just for one post. I googled "free blog" and came across Medium, a writing platform I had heard of in passing but completely forgotten about. Within minutes, I created a free account and posted my first article titled, *A Letter to My Middle School Bully.*

As soon as I clicked publish, my shoulders dropped and I released a breath I had been holding for nearly two decades.

18

BEHIND THE FACADE

"Did you know I used to think about the middle school bullying almost every day? At least weekly?" I asked my mom via text message, going on to tell her that I hadn't thought about it in the three weeks since I published the article.

"Better than therapy. It's a declaration to the world," she replied.

After posting the letter, two things happened. First, I started physically healing in a way that I never expected. I've been a nail-biter my whole life. If I wasn't using my hands to write, type, or gesture while I was talking, I was biting—no, *gnawing*—on the tips of my fingers. More often than not, my nails were barely visible; overtaken by redness and infection, causing pain each time a small drip of water landed on them. Washing my hands was unbearable and hand sanitizer a form of torture.

Most of the time, I didn't even know I was biting until someone, typically my husband, called me out with a subtle cough, strong glare, or an, "I see you biting over there, love bug," to pull me out of my trance. Over the years, I'd tried everything to break the habit: getting weekly manicures, carrying around nail clippers, using nibble inhibitors, the nail polish that tastes like poison, and even going to a hypnotist. Nothing worked... until I posted the letter to my middle school bully. In the weeks after I shared the post, I didn't bite my nails *at all*. It wasn't purposeful; I just didn't have the urge to bite. Instead, I looked down every few minutes, watching in awe as my nails grew longer and stronger into a length I hadn't seen in years.

"The weirdest thing happened," I told my mom, also a biter, over the phone one afternoon.

"Ever since I posted the blog, I haven't bitten my nails. They got so long that I had to clip them last night!" I exclaimed in joy.

"I'm in shock," she said. "I've never known you to clip your nails."

"I know," I replied. "It's so strange."

For the life of me, I couldn't figure out why sharing this specific post made me stop biting, but I ran with it, enjoying having healthy nails for the first time in my adult life. Painting my nails became an enjoyable activity instead of a chore; I could finally—*finally!*—open a soda can without asking for help; and I could scratch my own shoulder when I had an itch instead of squirming in discomfort and frustration. I experienced so many little joys I had never experienced before, all because I clicked "Publish" on a 1,413-word blog post.

Could biting my nails have been a sign I was holding onto the bullying? I wondered. I had been biting since I was a little girl—middle school age, at least. *Was it a sign I was harboring unresolved trauma?*

In addition to physical healing, the prior three weeks had shown me the power of writing as a form of therapy.

The day after I published the letter to my middle school bully, I wrote about something I had been struggling with my entire adult life—labeling myself. When I created my Medium account, I was asked to create a 160-character bio that would be shown at the bottom of every post. I thought about how, over time, I molded myself to embody and become the person who was described in my Instagram bio. Given my bio was a tool to get others to click the follow button, it was a curated version of how I wanted others to see me. I morphed into the person I described at the top of my feed—someone who chose a healthy lifestyle and loved sunrise walks, coffee shops, farmers markets, and yoga. It was me, but it wasn't *me*. After writing about the tug-of-war to be someone I wasn't, I came to the conclusion that my new bio was "I am who I am," a phrase from the Torah that stuck with me since I first read the passage in Hebrew school, well over a decade earlier.

Two days after publishing that post, I wrote about my meditation journey and how I meditated for ninety days straight. A few days later, I published an article about faith; something I had never talked about online before. The following week, I posted a list inspired by a gratitude practice my mom told me about. I titled the piece, *The first sip of coffee + 99 other small things that bring me joy*, with a simple subtitle: *the title says it all.*

With each post, I felt a little lighter, but I also started to feel the rising pressure that comes with creating content online. *If you put effort into writing, don't you want people to see it?* I asked myself again and again. After closing down my Lauren Lives Healthy and Wandering in Wellness channels, I didn't have any platforms to promote my posts on, so I resorted to LinkedIn, a place I had never shared blogs or content before because I was worried about what my former, current, and future colleagues would think of my overly personal writing style. I had an existing audience on the platform and wasn't ready to build one from scratch again, so LinkedIn seemed like a good place to start.

On average, each post was seen by more than fifteen hundred people, and with each like and comment, I started to feel the dopamine running through my blood at full speed. To keep the high going, I kept writing. I wrote every day, aiming to post as often as possible.

On May 4, 2021, I sent my mom a text message:

You sparked another (long-term) idea. I feel like I'm using my writing on Medium to heal. When I get to a point where I feel like I've shared my full story, I might print it out—like a book or collection of essays, just for myself. I could call it Better than Therapy: How sharing my story online helped me heal. I could leave it on my desk or bookshelf as a physical reminder of everything I've been through and overcome. Putting this idea on the back burner for sure.

I spent every waking hour over the next two days creating a Medium publication, a space for stories written around a common theme. I called it "Better than Therapy," a nod to the earlier conversation with my mom. I created a logo and had what I thought was a genius idea to create a podcast of the same name. Talking has always been a form of therapy for me, so maybe if I read the articles aloud, I could connect with people on an even deeper level while continuing my own healing journey. I got everything set up, recorded my first podcast, and shared the link with my mom via text message. Within thirty minutes, she replied:

Lauren, be careful with that. Your experience is very valuable. But you're not a therapist. You can't use that tag line. Someone could misinterpret that you are. I think you risk getting sued by someone who is seriously mentally ill. This is not mom talking. This is a lawyer.

My excitement drained instantly. I loved "Better than Therapy," but no one but me saw or understood the irony behind the name the way I did. After a lengthy conversation with my mom and my brother, who also raised concern about the name, I realized "Better than Therapy" was dangerous for others—and for myself. It conveyed thoughts like therapy isn't worth it, therapy is bad, and I don't need therapy when I was, in fact, an advocate for the practice. It took me some time to come around, but I eventually saw their perspective and realized I needed a new name.

Maybe it was the marketer in me, but the name of my passion projects was more than just a title. Because I was—and am—so invested in my projects and thought about them around the clock, the branding typically became more of an identity than a hobby for me. The name of the publication was something I'd think about or see every time I logged onto Medium or jotted down a note with an idea to explore in a future post. For something so personal and vulnerable, I wanted it to empower me to feel like I could be my authentic self and share whatever I wanted without a filter.

Feeling inspired but lost and overwhelmed with all the possibilities, I started looking back at my writing to see if anything resonated. In a yet-to-be-published story that talked about my most recent breakdown, I wrote:

> *Until that moment, I had been putting on my normal smile when I was around others, asking how they were and responding, "I'm fine," or, "Hanging in there," when they asked in return. I played off the comments about how tired I looked with, "Oh, I'm just sleep deprived. You know." But behind the facade, I was hanging on by a thread, on the verge of a breakdown that I knew was coming but didn't know when it would hit.*

Behind the facade. Was that it?

In another article, I wrote:

> *Everything I've shared online, and even with friends in person (until I joined Medium) had a veil over it. Like many, I wanted to appear to have the perfect life. If I posted a photo on Instagram, nine times out of ten, it had filters on it to make life seem brighter, clearer and more vivid than it really was. Sure, sometimes the smile you saw online was genuine, but other times it was completely forced, a photo fabricated for the sole purpose of being posted and shared.*

I couldn't stop thinking about it. *Behind the facade.*

From the title, readers could assume the stories would be real, raw, and vulnerable. When the words "behind the facade" popped into my head, they would remind me to write what's true and authentic to myself. The title also had some negative undertones, alluding to the sadness in my writing, but in a way, it was also uplifting, like I had the space to find myself. To grow.

I thought about it, I asked others for their opinions, and I slept on it. In the morning, I just knew: Behind the Facade was it.

Landing on this name inspired me to open up in a way I never thought I could or would before. In the post where I announced the new name, I wrote:

> I'm not sure why I want to put [my healing journey] out there for the whole world to see, but I think it's more important than ever to own who I am and convey that, even if someone is successful on paper, they may be silently struggling.
>
> I think it's because I need that when I'm in my dark seasons, but it's hard to find. At least in my experience, people don't really open up in [an honest and vulnerable] way—online or off. So by me opening up [like that], maybe I can be the friend to someone else that I wish I had.

Looking back at the surface-level content I previously shared online—meals, workouts, smiling selfies—I thought I'd be scared to put myself out there in such a raw way, but I felt just the opposite. I was empowered to share my true feelings in hopes they would inspire someone else to do the same.

It's not about you, my inner voice scolded me. *You're going right back to where you once were, creating content for other people. This time, it's just veiled as healing.*

I ignored the voice and kept writing, recording, and hitting publish. I was trying to prove to myself and others that I was okay, when really I wasn't. I was hiding behind yet another facade.

19

SLEEP FOREVER

"I'm fucking exhausted," I told my brain. "Please just let me sleep."

It had been six weeks straight without a full night's sleep, and I tried everything imaginable to induce rest. Medication, meditation, yoga, CBD, eliminating caffeine, avoiding naps, no technology at night, warm milk—you name it, I'd done it.

I got three, maybe four, hours of sleep per night if I was lucky. For someone who typically slept eight hours on the dot, I was holding on by a thread, constantly agitated, struggling to remember things, and thinking and moving like I was in slow motion. It was like I was drunk even though I hadn't had a sip of alcohol in years.

On top of the insomnia, my work life was out of control. I had recently been promoted and felt like I was working three jobs instead of the one I was promised. Every so often, I googled "Oregon stress leave," wondering if it would be possible to take time off to force my mind to be quiet and get some sleep. It required a doctor's note, which I was confident I could get.

The last time I went through a similar but shorter bout of insomnia, the doctor prescribed sleeping pills and medication. I could only imagine how they would react when they saw the massive bags under my eyes and the exhaustion seeping through my skin. If history were to repeat itself, and I had a teary breakdown in the doctor's office, I was confident they would support me. I was a mess, figuratively and literally.

I didn't want to jeopardize my career by taking a leave of absence. I knew people who had taken stress leave, and I was intimately familiar with the stigma around mental health in the workplace. In my experience, colleagues, managers and human resources reps don't often react the same way to mental illness as they do to a physical injury. Plus, I couldn't afford to take unpaid or subsidized time off. Not to mention, my team was in one of the busiest seasons of the year, amplified by the uncertainty of the COVID-19 pandemic, so it didn't feel right to pursue extended leave.

One day, though, I reached my limit, and yet again searched "stress leave" on the company's internal portal, taking note of the forms and processes I would have to go through. Rather than being excited about the prospect of not working for two, three, or four months, I was sad. I loved my job and as a live-to-work kind of person, I couldn't imagine not working for an extended period of time. By the time I logged into my next virtual meeting, a one-on-one with a senior executive I had started supporting the month before, my eyes were puffy, red, and swollen.

"Before diving in, do you mind if I ask you a personal question?" I asked hesitantly. I didn't know him well, but something about his demeanor made me trust him.

"Sure," he replied with a cautious smile, seemingly caught off guard.

"Do you ever get burned out?" I asked, knowing that, like me, he also had a number of roles, albeit at a higher level.

"Of course," he responded, "And if you are or ever get to that point, we need to talk about it." He went on to explain how he struggled to balance everything on his plate, sharing the human side that a leader typically doesn't show. I thanked him for being open and honest, sniffling along the way.

"I don't want to make any assumptions," he said carefully, "but it looks like you've been crying. Are you okay?"

I'm usually happy and professional on work calls, forcing a smile and responding, "I'm great," when people ask how I'm doing, but I just couldn't do it anymore. The idea of sending or receiving one more email or taking on one more project was too much to handle. I responded honestly, telling him how burned out I was. I mentioned how much the lack of sleep was getting to me, but it was more than that. The unexpected amount of work that came with a recent promotion, limited support from my manager, and a myriad of other challenges in the workplace all added up.

"It's clear you need a break," he said when I was done rambling. "I really think you should take tomorrow and Friday off. In fact, what do you have going on this afternoon? Can you log off now?"

I listed off a couple of meetings I had that afternoon, the most pressing of which was a group call that he would be in too.

"Don't worry, I've got it covered," he assured me. "What else?"

We reached our allocated time, but he stayed on the phone with me for fifteen extra minutes as I cleared my calendar and apologized profusely.

"Stop apologizing," he said multiple times. "I'm here to support you."

As soon as we got off the phone, I cleared my calendar and secured coverage for the unlikely event that any immediate requests would come in during my absence. I sent a note to my manager, telling her I'd be out for the rest of the week with reassurance that nothing urgent should pop up and, if it did, the team had it covered. I said I'd catch her up the following week and logged off, taking the executive's instructions to go lie on the couch. I didn't fall asleep, but it didn't matter. Getting permission to rest—and breathe—was all I needed.

I'd never received support like that before in a professional setting and definitely not from a senior leader. I was used to managing everything myself; doing so was part of my role as a communications partner. The one time I asked my manager for support prioritizing my workload, I received eye rolls and frustration in return. Ever since that experience, I avoided inconveniencing my superiors like the plague.

Even though I was forcing my body to slow down, my mind was still racing. I called my brother, telling him that I felt like I was going 180 miles per hour and couldn't stop, much less slow down.

"Lauren," he told me over the phone, "you're not a Prius that's designed to go the speed limit. You are a race car. Race cars are high-performance vehicles that are built to go at very high speeds. But the thing is, race cars can't race without maintenance and care. If you are a solar-powered race car and your solar panels aren't working, energy isn't going into the vehicle so it can't do anything. Plus, race cars have a pit crew to help keep it in tip-top shape; they rely on other people to change the tires, check on the engine, clean the windshield, etc. Right now, you need to focus on maintenance so you can get back to your race."

Damn, I thought. *I have one smart brother.*

After saying our goodbyes, I cozied up on the couch, binge watching crappy rom-coms on Netflix for the rest of the afternoon. At one point, I had the strange urge to write a haiku, a poem that contains three lines, alternating five, seven, and five syllables, coming together to form a seventeen-syllable poem. I opened my Notes app and typed:

Mind: please go to bed
I need rest more than you know
I beg of you, please

I sent the poem to my mom, who I had been texting with nonstop all afternoon.

"I'll do one," she replied. "This is fun!"

For me, it wasn't fun; it was an act of desperation. I wondered if, perhaps, poetry was the secret connection to the area of my brain that regulated sleep. I didn't know and I didn't care. I was willing to try anything. I went to bed with high hopes that I'd *finally* get a full night of sleep, thanks to my lazy afternoon.

Like clockwork, I woke up at 2:00 a.m. after just three hours of sleep. Trying not to wake my husband or dog, I tip-toed downstairs and curled up on the couch. While the haiku didn't work the first time, it gave me something to do to pass the time, so I wrote another one.

There's so much pressure
I am tired; it's all too much
When is it enough?

As soon as I finished that poem, I wrote a third, then a fourth, and then a fifth. The words just poured out of me in seventeen-syllable increments. Over the course of the next four hours, I thought about love, loss, grief, and everything in between, documenting my rollercoaster of emotions in the form of haiku. By the time 6:00 a.m. rolled around, I had a list of fifty poems. On Wednesday, May 12 at 6:02 a.m., I sent my mom an email, joking that I wrote my first book:

In this collection of fifty haiku, written in the early predawn hours of May 12, 2021, debut poet Lauren Bartleson expresses the thoughts that race through the millennial's mind, keeping her from sleep.

With just three lines and a total of seventeen syllables each, her poetry is a raw, realistic look at how the pressure of doing it all—balancing marriage, friendships, family, work, self-care, social media and societal expectations, all while living through a global pandemic, a mental health crisis and a loneliness epidemic—can bubble up to a breaking point.

It is an honest and vulnerable look into the mind of a twenty-something who's on a journey to answer one of life's most asked questions: Can you do it all?

I laughed to myself as I reread the blurb, proud for turning a sleepless night into something productive. Under the description, I pasted the list of fifty-three-line poems before hitting send. A couple hours later, I received a response: *Is this what you did all night? Omg!!*

After conversing with my mom via email for a few minutes, I felt an overwhelming need to sleep wash over me. I lay down on the couch, my eyes heavier than they had ever felt before. I pulled a blanket over me and closed my eyes, ready to fall into a deep, deep sleep. I tossed and turned in frustration, the morning light shining through our big glass windows keeping me from sleep.

I needed a dark room where I could be alone and fall into a deep black hole where I could never come out. In a zombie-like state, I made my way upstairs to our guest room, which was a significantly smaller space than our primary bedroom and faced away from the sunrise, much to my satisfaction. I got into bed and fell asleep as soon as my head hit the pillow, the sunlight blocked by the blinds we inherited from the previous owner. I fell into a deep slumber, the kind where, when you try to wake up, you can't open your eyes.

Even so, I tried to open my eyes again once my mind started waking up. They were super-glued shut, unwilling and unable to open, even a peek. I reasoned with myself: I'd try twice, and then I could let go.

I can die here, in my sleep, I told myself. *I've lived a good life and have felt more love than I ever hoped for.*

I thought of the influencer who died by suicide, and honestly? I was kind of jealous. In that moment, sleeping forever seemed much more appealing than living, even for one more minute.

Unable to open my eyes, I fell back asleep, determined to make my dark thoughts come to fruition. To my dismay, my mind woke up what felt like minutes later, though it could have been seconds or hours. I'll never know. Yet again, I tried to open my eyes but couldn't, the cycle repeating itself as I fell back asleep yet again.

The third time it happened, I was convinced I not only wanted to die but I *needed* to die—not because I was afraid of living but because I wanted an infinite amount of sleep. As I lay, I thought about my family—Matt, Georgia, my parents, my brother—and realized I couldn't do it. I couldn't hurt them.

I willed myself to open my eyes but nothing happened. Despite growing up Jewish, I struggled to grasp the idea of God and never really prayed. In this moment, I did what I imagined was something like praying, where you're begging and pleading for something and you have to wait for what you asked for to happen on someone else's terms. While I waited, I thought about those who had impacted my life and wondered if I impacted theirs in return.

I thought of my aunt and how much her death impacted my mom.

I thought of my grandfather I never got to meet.

I thought of the influencer who died by suicide, who would never get to experience life or love or loss or happiness or joy on Earth again.

I realized I wanted to live, but in order to do so, I had to open my eyes. Step one.

I'm not exaggerating. Opening my eyes was one of the hardest things I've ever done. Truly, I was hovering between wanting to sleep forever and wanting to get up. They were pulling me in two opposite directions, like a rope that's being pulled so tightly during a tug-of-war that it rips right down the middle.

In the end, I found the strength to open my eyes. As soon as I did, I rolled over and put my feet on the floor, making myself stand up before the blankets pulled me back into that dark place. I genuinely don't think I've ever exerted that much physical or mental energy in my entire life. It took every ounce of energy I had to open my eyes, to stand up, and to convince myself to walk downstairs.

At this point, it was late morning with sunlight pouring into the hallway. I moved slowly, each step feeling like I was dragging a stack of bricks behind me. A journey that typically takes ten seconds took me minutes, my mind fighting for me to go back to bed—to the safety of darkness—but my body and heart pushing me downstairs toward love.

When I got to my husband's office, I knocked quietly and, upon entering, gave him a hug, weak in nature but filled with all the strength I could muster. I told him how tired I was, that I was going to go lie on the couch. I didn't tell him what happened. I couldn't. I didn't want to scare him or, more importantly, make my feelings real.

At one point he came out to the living room to check on me, and I asked if he was worried.

"We all are," he said, mentioning that my mom texted him, asking him to check in on me. Little did he know, the moment he came into the room was probably around the time I was at my lowest, giving myself permission to let go.

For the next few hours, I put on a facade, texting friends and family like everything was normal. I didn't want pity or sympathy from anyone—not other people or myself. Eventually, putting on a front got to be too much, though. Late that afternoon, I broke down in tears as I told my husband about the thoughts that swirled through my head earlier that morning. As I told him about the negative thoughts that came and stayed, pulling me deeper and deeper into the abyss, I realized I wasn't scared of dying. I was scared of hurting those I love. I was afraid he would clam up and go into a shell, but, instead, he pulled me in close.

"I'm scared," he whispered in my ear, both of us afraid to talk too loudly.

"Me too," I whispered back, snuggling into his shoulder as close as I possibly could.

20

THE ANXIETY IS REAL

Before I knew it, tears were streaming down my face. I was breathing hard, my body not having enough energy to move, much less cry, until that moment.

For the first time in days, I was doing the dishes. I washed a pot, a lid, and a spatula before I had to drop the sponge, unable to see past the flowing tears.

"What's happening?" I wondered aloud in desperation, even though I was the only one in the kitchen. "I'm just trying to do the dishes for God's sake."

I collapsed on the floor, trying to breathe my way through the heart palpitations and bleary eyes. My cheeks started burning while my legs started shaking. I fell to the floor, settling into a ball on the mat in front of the sink. Although it felt like hours, it only took a few minutes for my nerves to calm enough that I could stand and make my way to the couch.

All I wanted to do was clean the kitchen, I scolded myself.

Why couldn't I even manage that? I thought disappointingly.

Dirty dishes had been sitting in the sink for the better part of a week, crusty pots and pans from meals past still on the stovetop and stale crumbs from dinner the prior week covering the counter. For months, my silent motto had been, "When the kitchen is clean, my mind is clean," so seeing our kitchen that messy and not having the energy to do anything about it felt like a failure—as a homeowner, a human, and most importantly, a wife. All I wanted to do was finish the freaking dishes. Why was it so hard?

Matt walked out from his office, completely unaware of the breakdown that just happened in the next room. We had been walking around on eggshells for two weeks; him worried that I'd do something to hurt myself and me scared that he'd worry himself to death. Every ten minutes, he'd ask how I was doing; if I was okay; if I needed anything. With each question, the bags under his eyes got darker and darker, and his voice sounded less and less chipper, like he could no longer force himself to be happy and upbeat for my sake. I didn't want to burden him further, so I didn't ask for help in any way, shape, or form, even for something as small as doing the dishes. Instead, I kept promising him—and myself—that I'd do them.

Ignoring his: "How's it going, love?" I asked for a hug and apologized for not cleaning the kitchen.

"I only had energy for a few dishes," I explained. "I'll do the rest later. I promise."

"It's okay," he replied, fully knowing I wouldn't finish that night. I had been repeating the same apology and promise for four days straight, leaving the dishes for me to do. For the first eight years together, we didn't see eye to eye on who did dishes; he often felt like he cleaned up after me and vice versa, so I was determined not to make him feel that way in light of everything I was already putting him through. Each time he neared the overflowing sink, I'd stop him by saying, "Don't worry about the dishes," and force him to leave the kitchen dirty and disgusting, mirroring how grimy and useless I felt on the inside.

"When you finish the dishes," he said, "I'll do the counters."

He gave me a kiss on the cheek before heading back to his office. As soon as he left, I sauntered back over to the sink, willing myself not to let the tears come back.

I put on a playlist I had been listening to nonstop and got to work. I had put together a collection of nineteen songs to get me through moments exactly like this, when I felt like life was too much to handle. With music playing in the background, I slowly but surely made it through the entire stack of dishes. I also cleaned the counters, even though Matt said he'd do it. I convinced myself I needed to make up for the mess I'd made that week, both physically and emotionally. When the kitchen was spotless and glistening, the freedom engulfed me. I took a deep breath, letting air flow through my lungs and into my belly. I sighed it out, relieved. It was over. Whatever just happened, it was over. I could breathe again.

I made my way to the couch and pulled out my phone to call my mom. Since I told her about the middle school bullying experience, we had been talking on a near-daily basis on the phone, in addition to our daily text messages.

"How are you?" she asked once we said our quick hellos.

"Well to be totally honest, I just had a breakdown while doing dishes," I started. Things like this aren't off-limits anymore; we talked openly about everything, especially my mental health, even if it was uncomfortable.

"I don't know what's happening to me," I told her, my eyes starting to water as I went on. "Why am I even crying over the dishes anyway? It's so stupid."

"Lauren," she said gently. "You can't live like this."

She was right. I knew she was, but I still didn't know what to do. I was trapped in a cycle of breakdowns, crying for no reason before retreating to the couch or bed and not getting up for hours on end, and then doing it all again. In an atypical fashion, I was taking a mid-day nap every single day, the only saving grace getting me through the afternoon. I was struggling to focus, felt unmotivated at work, and was tired every second of every day. I thought back to the conversation with my husband the night before when I promised I would make an appointment to see my primary care physician.

Maybe this is another sign, I thought before dialing the doctor's office.

When I dialed in to my virtual appointment the following Tuesday, five days later, I was greeted not only by my doctor and her nurse but by a woman with light brown, almost red hair. She wore glasses and a smile.

Did she dial into the wrong call? I wondered. I had never seen this woman before and didn't recognize her name, but my doctor didn't say anything, so neither did I.

"So," my doctor started. "Tell me what's going on."

Word vomit spilled out of me:

"Despite implementing a nighttime routine like we talked about, I've been having trouble staying asleep. For the last seven weeks, I've been getting a max of four hours of sleep per night. This happened before—about two years ago—but lasted only six weeks. During that time, I took sleeping medication to help, which is what pulled me out of that stupor. I happened to have two pills left, so I took them both last night: one before going to sleep and one upon waking and not being able to fall back asleep. I can't pinpoint a trigger for it, but I have a feeling it has to do with switching antidepressants while simultaneously starting phentermine. I stopped the phentermine after clearing it with the endocrinologist. Not getting sleep is affecting everything, even work—so much so that I was told to take a few days off last week because I was so high-strung. After that, I had an experience where I felt like it would be better to sleep forever, which is what caused me to make this appointment. My husband encouraged me to call you when I told him about it."

I took a deep inhale, trying to catch my breath. She asked a few questions in return:

"Do you have plans to commit suicide?"

"No, but I think about death a lot."

"Do you snore when you sleep?"

"A little, but mostly when I'm sick."

"Have your legs been restless recently?"

"Only when I'm anxious."

"Looking at the questionnaire you did with my assistant before connecting," she started, "it looks like your depression is moderately severe and anxiety is severe."

"Let's see here," she said as she clicked around on her computer. "When you answered the same questions two months ago, your depression and anxiety scores were both mild."

"We have a couple of options," she said. "We can change the dosage of the current medication you're on, or we can go back to the one we started earlier in the year."

"What do you recommend?" I asked, inundated by the options she was throwing at me.

"If I were in your shoes," she said, "I'd go back on the other medication. Your numbers seemed to be good when we checked in a few months ago." That was Matt's first thought, too.

"Okay," I said. "Can you give me anything to help me sleep?" My eyes filled with tears and my voice trembled as I started to beg. "I'm tired. *So* tired. I'll take anything."

"I'll prescribe you trazodone," she agreed. "If you look it up, it'll say it's used to treat depression, but many physicians, me included, use it to treat sleep." I didn't care what the small print said; I would take anything I could get my hands on to start feeling more rested.

"I'll put in that order so you can pick it up at the pharmacy later today. I highly recommend you connect with a psychiatrist or psychologist. In the meantime, we have a social worker here to support you. Is there anything else you need from me before I leave you two to chat?"

What? Why do I need to talk to a social worker? I realized then who the other person in the call was.

I shook my head, unable to form a response. After a few seconds, I said, "Thank you," and that was that.

"Hi, Lauren," the woman said in a quiet voice, just above a whisper. I had to lean into the computer to hear what she was saying.

"I'm a social worker and partner with physicians in the building when they have patients, like you, who need a little extra care."

We spent the next twenty minutes chatting, her asking questions about my work, my relationship, and my family while I gave as simple of answers as possible. I was caught off guard, not at all ready to share my life story with someone I had never met and who talked to me in the same voice a parent used to console a two-year-old in the middle of a tantrum. She told me she would be my point of contact while I looked for a psychologist or psychiatrist and, as a social worker, she could provide interim therapy services.

"Before we log off, let's book a follow-up appointment for two weeks out. Can you be available first thing on June second?" It didn't seem like she'd take no for an answer, so I replied, "I'll make it work," and clicked off.

When the bill arrived in the mail, I was shocked to see it was $175 for the twenty minutes I spent with the social worker—on top of the $163.76 I owed for just ten minutes with my doctor. In just five months, I had spent a total of $2,130.38 on doctor's visits after insurance, and all I had to show for it was two new medications that caused insomnia and amplified my anxiety, depression, and suicidal thoughts.

That's it, I thought, while gritting my teeth in frustration. *We're moving to Canada.*

It took two days to find the courage to type "psychologytoday.com" into my browser. *Psychology Today* was the site I used to find my last therapist, and this time, I was determined to find someone covered by my insurance, unable and unwilling to fork over my ten grand out-of-pocket maximum for therapy services. I filtered down the options to those covered who focused on depression in my immediate location and promptly started reaching out to each of them. In order to get this done as quickly as possible, I copied and pasted the same exact message to over a dozen practitioners.

For the next twenty-four hours, I checked my email every ten minutes, feeling defeated each time I saw a response come in. Every single practitioner I reached out to said they were not taking on new clients due to the overflow from COVID-19. Some offered to put me on a waitlist, but I didn't have months to wait. By this point, I was experiencing suicidal thoughts on an hourly basis and needed help as soon as possible.

In desperation, I reached out to the therapist I saw the previous year:

It's been a while. I hope you're doing well. I wanted to see if you had time for an old patient.

To be completely honest, it's been a very rough few months in terms of mental health, and I had some very dark thoughts a few weeks ago. While I'm feeling a little better now, I think it would be smart to do a few sessions if you can make the time.

Do you happen to have any availability in the next week or two to dive back in? Looking forward to hearing from you.

I took his first available appointment three weeks later, eager to reconnect with a friendly face and skip over all the introductions and niceties.

21

WRITING INSOMNIA

I didn't admit to anyone—not my husband, not my mom, not even the doctor—how often the negative thoughts occurred. I visualized scenario after scenario in my head, wondering each morning if that day would be my last.

On the three-minute drive to and from the supermarket, I'd think about swerving into oncoming traffic but couldn't fathom the idea of potentially taking someone else's life along with my own. Anything with a car was out. Each time I drove over the train tracks about a mile from our house, I thought about parking and sitting on the tracks, waiting for a freight train to come barreling toward me at full speed, but that wasn't an option either. I had read articles talking about the train conductors on the other side who suffered from PTSD, and I couldn't put someone and their family through that. I thought of alcohol, but couldn't stomach the thought of it, much less the taste or smell. No way would I be able to drink more than a sip without getting sick first.

My safest bet was pills. I had no problem downing a handful of Tylenol—pain killers never seemed to help, so I often took two to three times the suggested dosage, a tip I learned from my dad at a young age—and

I assumed sleeping pills wouldn't be any different. I had a prescription and kept an extra bottle on hand just in case, but I never took it upstairs, unable to bear the thought of hurting those I loved most by hurting myself. Instead, when the negative thoughts took over, I sat down on the couch and started writing.

I still had a few weeks before my therapy appointment, so I wrote about all the things I wished I could tell my therapist: how exhausted I was, how alone I felt, and how much I was struggling to manage my COVID-19 anxiety. I wrote about the hourly panic attacks I experienced, how social media exacerbated my thoughts, what was getting me through those dark moments, and more. My writing, often inspiring and hopeful, turned dark.

"What are you doing?" my husband asked one night as he walked up behind me.

"Nothing," I answered, quickly closing my laptop. I wasn't quick enough, though. He caught the words, *What my obituary would say*, in big, bold letters before I shut my computer.

Other than what happened on the morning I wanted to sleep forever, my husband had no idea I was experiencing negative thoughts on a regular basis. I was too scared to tell him the truth, afraid it would turn into an argument, or worse, disappointment. I avoided disappointing him at all costs, so instead I became an actor playing a part, acting as normal as I could for his sake.

When he asked me why I was writing about what my obituary would say, I froze. I looked up at him, my eyes locked as if I were a deer caught headlights. Instead of using this as an opportunity to open up to him, I played it off with a laugh, turning away so he couldn't see the tears welling in my eyes. I never admitted to him—or anyone—how often I thought about my obituary. Other than my career in marketing and communications, I wasn't sure I could possibly be remembered for anything else. I was nothing special—a tiny fish in the big corporate sea. Even preparing for death, all I cared about was what other people thought of me. I ignored his follow-up questions, willing him to leave with silence. I wasn't ready to have that conversation or feel the deep regret and disappointment that would bubble up to the surface if I let them.

Each morning, I woke up feeling hung over and sleep deprived, despite taking the sleeping pills religiously. Opening my eyes was the ultimate challenge. After blinking them open and getting a quick glimpse of the early morning sunlight peeking through our blinds, I closed them tightly again. Before I could fall back asleep, the neighborhood rooster's cock-a-doodle-doo hit my ears, a sound way too loud that early in the morning. Like clockwork, I'd throw off the duvet in frustration and huff to the bathroom, giving myself a mental pep talk along the way.

Every morning was the same: bright light, rooster, pep talk. All I had to do was make it to the next morning, and I knew I'd be okay. That damn rooster would never let me sleep.

I needed a project to keep me busy during the day, something to pull me away from the negative thoughts. I thought back to the collection of poems I sent my mom, joking that I wrote a book.

How cool would it be if I actually did that? I mused.

I had two problems: I wasn't a poet, and I wasn't sure how to publish a book.

I don't care, I told myself as I brought up Google, ready to tackle both items.

I started by thinking about the content. I had the fifty haiku already, but that wasn't enough for me. As a long-form writer, I needed some form of context behind each of those poems. Unsure of where to start, I googled "haiku with other text."

One word popped up in every response—prose. I'd heard the word before but didn't know what it meant. As I started reading about prose poetry, I learned that it's a form of poetry that, unlike the typical poetry I saw on Instagram, wasn't broken into verses or lines, yet still used symbols, metaphors, and other figures of speech common to poetry.

That could work, I thought, bringing up a new tab to do more research.

"Haiku and prose," I typed into the search bar. Right below the title of the first search result, I read, "Haibun is a poetry form that combines a haiku with a prose poem. Haibun prose is usually descriptive."

That's it! I exclaimed in my head as a smile started to form on my face.

As I read more about this new-to-me poetry form, I learned that haibun originated in Japan and often talked about everyday events and happenings while haiku focused on nature. Haibun didn't have strict guidelines like haiku's seventeen-syllable requirement, just freedom to write as long as it included at least one haiku.

In my Notes app, I found the document with the long list of haiku and wrote my first piece of prose:

Legs shaking, mind racing. Sleep little, rise when the clock strikes three. Six weeks and counting with no end in sight. It's time: I'm asking for help—from the body, the mind, the doctor. Hello? Anyone? Can you hear me?

I had never read, much less written prose, but I was pretty damn happy with what poured out of me in those sixty seconds. For the first time in weeks, maybe even months, I felt a purpose. I had to keep writing.

I worked my way down the list, writing one piece of prose for each haiku, giving more subtle context to the emotions I felt in each poem. As I kept writing, the book came alive in my Notes app. The words poured out of me, and before I knew it, I had ten, then twenty, then fifty pieces of prose along with the haiku.

The next day, I sat in on a virtual comedy-meets-poetry event about mental health. I watched in awe as the two hosts talked openly about their mental health experiences, including how they thought about and overcame suicidal thoughts. Toward the end of their ninety-minute virtual event, they shared a few tools and resources that helped them manage anxiety.

One of the first tactics they introduced was naming your emotions. They talked about the power of identifying a feeling like anger or frustration, rather than trying to push through the unknown, and encouraged viewers to download an emotion wheel to use as reference. Before that moment, I genuinely never thought to associate what I was feeling with a specific emotion. Instead, like many others, I just let what I was feeling wash over me and try to wade through the myriad of emotions, often failing out of confusion and overwhelm.

After the event, I sent the two hosts a thank you note, letting them know that they were helping me through a tough time and promised to look into the emotion wheel. One of the hosts replied with a link to the wheel they used, so I opened it in my browser and had a thought: *What if I include this in my book as a way to remind myself of the power of naming my emotions? I could name each haibun a different emotion from the wheel, showing how many emotions I felt in the night leading up to one of my darkest moments.*

I printed out the wheel and walked straight downstairs to get to work. I re-read each poem, thinking back to how I felt in the moment I wrote it. At the top of each page, I wrote a corresponding word from the wheel:

Anxious.

Exhausted.

Depressed.

Powerless.

Hopeful.

Jovial.

Within minutes, I added another powerful layer to the book and was thrilled with how it was starting to come together. Along with the poems, I had already written the dedication, preface, introduction, author's note, and acknowledgments. All I had to do now was edit it.

I wanted this book to be as authentic as possible, so I didn't linger on each word like I normally would. I wrote the first words that came to mind, the same way I had when I wrote each haiku, and that's what I wanted to document. Every project I did—Instagram, the blog, writing on Medium—was to share my writing with other people. Other than a couple of journal entries that I forgot to post, I had never written just for me, and I was craving having something, a secret, that was my own.

Me being me, I couldn't put my name on something that wasn't perfect. My mother-in-law, a published author who had edited multiple books, offered to edit my work if I ever chose to publish a book. I tentatively messaged her, telling her my idea and asking if she would read and edit my book for me before I sent it to the printer.

"Please don't worry," I added at the end of my text message. "I'm doing okay right now."

"Thank you for saying that. I would have been worried," she replied almost immediately. "I would be honored to edit for you. Send it over."

Within hours, I received a text saying that she took a first pass and that she was bawling the whole time. She promised to come back to what I had been calling *Insomnia* the next day for proper editing.

I landed on the name *Insomnia* early on in the writing process when I started drawing out a mock-up for the cover. I wanted a five-syllable word with dots breaking up the syllables, a nod to the syllable requirement of each line in haiku. The only word that kept popping into my mind was insomnia, which was perfect despite only having four syllables. The whole purpose of the book was to document the emotions I felt over the course of one sleepless night, and what could describe that better than the word *insomnia*? It stuck.

From the get-go, my goal was to publish one copy that would live on my bookshelf as a reminder of how strong and resilient I was; that I was brave enough to go out of my comfort zone, creative enough to write poetry, driven enough to design the interior and cover, and determined enough to figure out how to publish it myself.

After finalizing the content thanks to my mother-in-law's edits, I started looking into how to actually turn my Word document into a printed book—just in time for my first therapy appointment.

I walked into the appointment feeling proud of myself for the first time in months, proceeding to tell the counselor about the progress I made writing and podcasting, despite not having access to professional support since my breakdown. After mentioning my book and my plan to print only one copy and not promote it, he replied with a quick, "Don't discount yourself. Your story could help others."

I thought back to the influencer's death and the thousands of comments talking about struggling with anxiety, depression, and suicidal thoughts. *Could my book—and by proxy, me—be the friend to them that she was to me in my darkest moments?*

"You're right," I responded. I needed to publish my book—not just for me, but for others who may be struggling as much as I was.

22

PUBLISHING INSOMNIA

The idea of publishing a book wasn't new to me.

Four years prior, I was managing the LinkedIn presence of a senior executive at a leading technology company. During one of our regular check-ins, I asked if I could share an idea with him to get his initial feedback.

"I'm thinking of writing an ebook," I started, going on to explain how I wanted to turn what I did for him and other leaders—managing their digital presence on their behalf—into a PDF that leaders of all levels could use to improve their presence on social media.

"I really like the idea," he started, "but I think you should consider doing a print or Kindle book, too. That way, leaders can read it on the plane when they're traveling." As an executive at one of the world's leading technology companies, he was my target market, so I took his feedback and recommendation seriously. I made a note, design ideas already swirling through my head.

"How much does it cost to write and publish a book?" he asked.

"About sixty-five hundred dollars," I mumbled, thinking back to the google search I did when the idea first crossed my mind. At the time, sixty-five hundred dollars was equivalent to a million dollars on my salary, and I couldn't afford to cover the cost myself. Even so, I took a moment to envision a book with my name on it gracing *The New York Times* bestsellers list, a warmth instantly washing over me.

One day, I promised myself. *One day.*

As I came out of my daydream, I heard him smiling through the phone as he offered to fund 100 percent of the costs—out of his own pocket, not the company's.

Wait, *what? Did he just say what I thought he did?* My jaw dropped as the realization hit. I thanked him profusely, promising to get back to him with concrete numbers soon.

As soon as humanly possible, I went to the bookstore, assuming someone had to have written a book like this already. Out of Powell's Books sixty-eight thousand square foot "City of Books," they only had two books on LinkedIn. Two. I took it as a sign and immediately started writing the manuscript and researching publishers on top of creating a business plan to share back with my client.

I dove head-first into the process, reaching out to other authors I followed on Instagram to learn how they went about publishing their book. One replied with contact information for her agent and told me to send my query letter directly to her.

"What's a query letter?" I asked Google, proceeding to create a book proposal and query letter based on examples I found within the first few pages of search results. I sent it to a handful of literary agents with high hopes that I would get an immediate contract offer. No one responded.

When I sat down to write the manuscript, fear, nerves, and uncertainty kicked in. I convinced myself no one would read my work. I questioned whether, at twenty-six years old, I had the credibility and expertise to put my name on a business book. Every time I opened a blank document to start writing, I spent the entire time trying to pull myself out of a mental black hole and ended up writing next to nothing.

Eventually, I completed the query letter, including general information about the book, a description, a note about me as the author, and a quick thank you. I included the first fifteen pages, in hopes the hook would draw them in.

Thank you for reaching out, one automated response started. *I will need to pass on this manuscript at this time. I wish you luck with future submissions.*

My excitement quickly turned sour, my bruised ego feeling like the end of the world rather than a temporary ache. After receiving one too many form rejection letters and, worse, no response at all, I gave up on the project all together. I was too ashamed to tell the executive, so I severed our relationship, going from communicating regularly to ad hoc LinkedIn messages saying, "happy birthday" or "congratulations on the new job." Avoidance, mirrored as lack of interest, was my standard response to not feeling wanted or good enough.

Despite physically moving on, the idea kept popping into my head, like an annoying gnat that never leaves, even when you swat it away. Here and there, I would pick the project back up, but after a couple hours—maybe a couple days, if I was lucky—I would end up back where I started, staring at a blank page with no motivation to write and imposter syndrome taking full control.

As I was scrolling LinkedIn one morning in April 2021, I saw a post from a colleague giving an update about the book she was writing. *A book?* I was instantly captivated, itching to learn more about the publishing route she chose. I sent her a message introducing myself, and we agreed to chat later that week.

She told me about a two-part writing program she was taking, which took place over two back-to-back semesters. The first half of the class had an ambitious but somewhat reasonable goal of writing a full-length manuscript in twenty weeks, and the second half guided you through the publishing portion. Throughout the program, she explained, you were paired with a variety of editors and cover designers who helped turn your idea to a real-life book that you could hold in your hands and buy from a bookstore.

"Would you like an introduction to the professor?" she asked, after hearing the history of my own book struggles.

"That would be great," I replied tentatively, nervous to commit to the book after such a long time. "Thank you so much."

On April 13, 2021, I sent an email to the professor, explaining my idea. I told him the book had been in the works for four years and I kept picking it up and putting it down. *If I'm being honest,* I wrote, *I'm worried that if I don't do it now, I never will.*

After a quick conversation via Zoom, the professor agreed my idea had real potential and, given I didn't have the patience—or, frankly, the thick skin—to attempt the traditional publishing process again, I moved forward. Their approach was different. In a hybrid model akin to guided self-publishing, authors received the guidance and support of a publisher while maintaining full rights and ownership of their book. I excitedly paid my deposit, started attending the weekly lectures, and met my first of many editors. A month in, however, everything came to a crashing halt when I had my insomnia-driven breakdown.

In my first therapy appointment, the psychologist and I talked openly about my struggle to manage work-life balance. I told him about a new mantra my friend and I came up with: 7:58, a promise to log off after being online for exactly seven hours and fifty-eight minutes, giving us two minutes of flexibility. I shared how proud I was that I was not only setting, but sticking to, boundaries. I celebrated working forty hours a week instead of my typical fifty-five, yet in the same breath, I complained how exhausted I felt, maybe even more so.

"Have you considered that maybe you're still working fifty-five hours a week if not more?" He asked.

Like a dog, I tilted my head in confusion, not sure where he was going with this.

"It sounds like you replaced the fifteen extra hours you were working with fifteen hours of writing or thinking about your book," he continued. "The topic is so closely related to what you do in your day job that your brain doesn't have a chance to shut off or switch gears. So even though you're working on something different, it's still contributing to your burnout."

Shit. He was absolutely right. I couldn't keep going this way.

After thinking about it for a few days, I sent my editor a message I was dreading:

I've made the difficult decision not to pursue the book we've been working on together. Given how burned out I am on the work front, I'm not in the mental space to write a book that's so closely aligned to what I do outside of office hours.

I had two options: stay in the class or drop out. I'm not a quitter so dropping out wasn't a real option. Instead, the question became which book would I write instead? I seriously considered *Insomnia,* but I didn't want to wait over a year to hold it in my hands. I needed to publish that book sooner rather than later so I could have it as a physical reminder if and when I wanted to sleep forever again. What if that was next week or next month? I couldn't risk it.

I decided to write a memoir in the class and self-publish *Insomnia* on my own timeline; the sooner I could get my hands on a copy of that book, the better. Within minutes, I was typing "How to self-publish a book" into my search bar, a jolt of natural energy hitting me like a shot of espresso. I couldn't find an all-encompassing guide for self-publishing a book, so I researched each step individually.

Over the next six hours, I scoured seemingly hundreds of sites, noting everything I would have to do to create a book from scratch. I read every blog I could find by self-published authors, detailed what they enjoyed, what they regretted, and what they wished they knew before publishing. For the first time in weeks, I felt an emotion other than depression; I was excited and energized by the challenge in front of me.

I started by narrowing down which form of publishing I wanted to use, opting for an on-demand printing service. This avenue would allow me to print just one copy for myself but would keep the door open in case I wanted to make the book more broadly available one day. Once I chose the distributor, I was able to decide details like book size and paper quality. I ran downstairs to grab a tape measure before walking to the bookshelf to grab my favorite poetry book as inspiration. *Paper size? Check.*

Next up—layout design. I'm a self-taught amateur graphic designer and wanted to put my skills to the test by designing both the interior layout and the cover myself. Again, I looked toward my favorite book as a guide for where to place my name, the book title and the page number on each page. I thought about which words I wanted capitalized, which I wanted italicized and in bold, and how many spaces needed to be between each title, prose, and haiku. *Interior layout? Check.*

I moved on to the cover, knowing that the design I chose could make or break the book. I already had a vision for the cover, so all I had to do was find a background image using a free stock image site and figure out how to create a design that flowed seamlessly from the cover to the spine to the back. Within hours, I had a design I loved. Even if I was the only person who would ever see this book, I wanted it to be perfect. I covered all my bases and left nothing behind.

The only thing left to do for the cover was get a barcode. From my research, that meant I had to buy a series of International Standard Book Numbers (ISBNs), which would be listed on the copyright page along with other small print. Unsure of where this book would go, I decided to buy three: one for the print book, one for the ebook, and a third for an audiobook. *Just in case*, I told myself. The ISBN assigned to the print book would be listed in the bar code, and I would print all three in the copyright area of the book. After a quick Google search for how to buy an ISBN, I quickly learned they were more expensive than I thought; however, there was a deep discount for buying ten ISBNs instead of purchasing each one individually.

I guess this means I'm self-publishing at least two more books, I thought as I entered my credit card number.

While I was at it, I figured out how to get a Library of Congress Control Number so my book could be included in the reading room if I chose to pursue that route one day.

By the time I submitted my book to the printer a mere week and a half later, I couldn't hold in my excitement. On July 12, 2021, two months to the day after I wanted to sleep forever, the book went live on Amazon and Barnes & Noble. I instantly added the book to my cart and proceeded to meticulously track my shipping information, eagerly awaiting my own copy to arrive. I nearly hugged the delivery driver when he handed me the small package two days later, tearing the bubble mailer open in the middle of our driveway, unable to get upstairs. I had the biggest smile on my face as I turned my book over in my hands for the first time.

"Look, love!" I shouted to my husband, even though he was barely a foot away from me. "I did it! I freaking did it."

It wasn't until six days later that I had the courage to promote it publicly, starting by sending an email to my family and friends before sharing it in a post on LinkedIn and Instagram. After thinking more about what my therapist had said, I realized that sharing my story could help break the stigma around mental health. Plus, it could help reinforce the idea that having anxiety doesn't mean you're a bad employee, having depression doesn't mean you're a negative person, and having dark thoughts doesn't mean you're unstable. It means you're human; all things I wholeheartedly believed even more after my breakdown.

I used the launch as an opportunity to raise money for mental health awareness by donating 100 percent of the royalties, the money after distributors and printers take their cut, to NAMI Washington County, my local chapter of the National Alliance on Mental Illness. NAMI is the nation's largest grassroots mental health organization and is dedicated to building better lives for the millions of Americans affected by mental illness. They offer a ton of resources, events, support groups, and hotlines for people of all ages who struggle with anxiety, ADHD, ADD, depression, bipolar, and other mental illnesses. Their Instagram had been a key source of support in the weeks I waited for my therapy appointment, and it meant so much to me that people chose to buy the book, in turn supporting an amazing organization.

From the get-go, my goal was to publish one copy of *Insomnia*, which would live on my bookshelf as a reminder of how strong and resilient I was; that I was brave enough to go out of my comfort zone, creative enough to write poetry, driven enough to design the interior and cover, and determined enough to figure out how to publish it myself. I was scared to put myself out there in such a vulnerable way, knowing that admitting to the world I struggled so much could impact my reputation, especially in the workplace, but I did it.

Not only was I a published author, I was a book designer, publisher, marketer, and publicist. *I freaking did it!*

23

SPIRALING, SPIRALING, SPIRALING

I was *done*. With work, life, everything. Writing and publishing *Insomnia* did its job; the project distracted me from feeling my feelings during the height of it all, but once I finished the book, reality came crashing down in full force.

On a sweltering Thursday in late May, I hit my breaking point. Work-related burnout, my dwindling friendships, the hot weather, my hair sticking to my neck... it suddenly all felt like too much.

I had an hour in between morning calls, so in the heat of the moment, I stomped downstairs to grab a pair of scissors before turning around and heading straight back up to our large bathroom. Without looking in the mirror, I chopped off an eight-inch section of hair. My otherwise long hair, which reached well below my shoulder blades, was part of my identity. Most days, I wore my hair in a loose bun but left it down for events and photos in an effort to feel and look more feminine. Although I had been thinking about cutting my hair for years, I never did. I always found an excuse to keep it long—so I could do a glamorous half-up, half-down hairstyle for my wedding, for example—but, in reality, I was too scared to chop it off, nervous of what other people would think. In that moment, however, I didn't care one bit what other people thought.

After the first chop, I felt a smile cross my face before it quickly turned into determination. I needed to be somewhat presentable for my upcoming video call, so I hurriedly grabbed another chunk of hair and cut off another eight-inch section. Then another, and then another. For forty-five minutes, I cut and cut, until the light gray, almost white marble floor was covered with dark brown curls. By the time I logged in to my next call, I had a laughably short, uneven bob with an unreasonable amount of hair covering my neck. I snapped a photo to document the moment and, despite my neck, chest, and arms being covered in hair, I was wearing the biggest, most authentic smile I had seen in weeks.

My parents came to visit the following day, and every couple of hours during their trip, I would excuse myself to go to the bathroom when I felt a stray piece of long hair that I forgot to cut. I'd slip away, make a few snips, and leave the scissors lying on the counter for the next time I found an out-of-place strand.

"I like your hair," my dad told me one afternoon as we were lying in the grass at the dog park.

"Thanks," I replied. "I like it, too."

I meant it. I loved the short length, even though the front was too long and the sides stuck out behind my ears. The short length was easy to maintain, wash, and dry, and, frankly, it made me feel like a badass. I regretted not cutting it sooner.

Over the next three days, I kept snipping, continuing to nit-pick at my hair until there was literally nothing left to cut. By Saturday, I had what looked like a nearly shaved head. Oddly enough, I felt the most confident I had in months. Years, even. Maybe even my whole life.

"What the hell did you do?" A close friend and coworker asked when we connected via Zoom the following week.

I shrugged. "I needed a change. Do you like it?"

"Honestly?" she asked. "I miss your long hair."

We had the type of friendship that went well beyond work, where we could be brutally honest without hurting each other's feelings. I took her comment for what it was— her opinion.

"It's just hair," I responded. "It'll grow back."

I genuinely didn't care what she or anyone else thought. After spending a lifetime trying to please others, it felt freeing to do something just for me. Something that wasn't planned or to meet anyone's standards. Something that showed myself—and the world—that I really didn't care about other people's opinions.

On top of the haircut, I started dressing differently— in one specific way. I had always wanted to work out in a sports bra but never felt like I could with my bigger body. In my *I don't give a fuck* mode, I figured why not try it out. I went to the gym wearing high-waisted leggings with a sports bra underneath my sweatshirt. After my warm-up, my face glistening with sweat, I peeled off my outer layer and set the sweatshirt beside the weight bench, nervously looking around to see if anyone was judging me. I picked up my dumbbells and finished my set of twelve chest presses before looking around again. No one noticed.

Truly, I don't think anyone cared what I was wearing; every other person in the gym was lost in their own world, counting reps, mouthing along to music, and focused on themselves. As I continued my workout, my confidence soared. I felt strong, proud that I wore what I wanted to wear, not what society implied bigger women should wear. I walked out of the gym drenched in sweat with a pep in my step.

Another thing I experimented with? Tattoos. I'd wanted one specific tattoo since high school: the Hebrew phrase that translated to "I am who I am," my new social media—and life—bio, which I envisioned on my inner left wrist. After hearing that people with tattoos can't be buried in Jewish cemeteries, a fact I later learned was incorrect, I worried I would be shunned from being with my loved ones after death. I was also extremely nervous that my family would judge me. In their eyes, I wasn't the "tattoo type," whatever that meant. Worse, I was worried my current and future employer would discount me for having visible tattoos. I was so afraid of being judged that I didn't do something I thought about every single day for years on end.

The weekend after chopping off my hair, I spent a few hours designing not one, but three, tattoos I envisioned: the "I am who I am" quote from a chapter of the Torah, when God meets Moses in the burning bush; Gigi's paw prints to remind me that love conquers all; and the title of my first book, *Insomnia*, a nod to the empowered feeling that came when I listened to my intuition over others' expectations.

Once I finalized the designs, I printed them out and cut out each individual tattoo, taping it to my skin where I pictured the design: the Hebrew phrase on my left inner wrist, Gigi's paw prints on my left palm, and in•som•ni•a on my inner right wrist, all facing me so I could see the reminders anytime I looked down. For almost two weeks, I repeated the process each time the paper and tape fell off, wanting to be absolutely sure I loved the content and placement before I permanently inked my skin. It would be months before I could get up the courage to walk into a parlor, but I was sure all three tattoos were happening.

The following week, I received messages from two different colleagues.

The first was a peer in India who I had worked closely with for nearly a year. When I started supporting the new executive, I had strict orders to stop partnering with this man and his team, so we went from talking on a daily basis to not at all. For the first time in months, we were in a meeting together. During the call, he messaged me via chat:

"Lauren," he wrote. "I'm worried. You chopped off all your hair, went MIA, and stopped posting on LinkedIn. Are you okay?"

I was touched that he not only noticed my haircut and the change in online behavior, but that he cared enough to ask. Asking someone if they're okay—and genuinely caring about their answer—goes a long way for someone who's struggling.

"Thank you for asking," I replied. "I'm going through a lot personally, but I'm hanging in there." I wasn't ready to get into all the details, especially with a colleague and even more so via chat, but I took the message to heart more than he'll ever know.

The second message came from an executive I supported in a former role, a woman I now considered a friend and a mentor.

She sent me a simple message: "Hope you are doing alright. Read some of your [LinkedIn] posts and wanted to check in and say hi." Knowing her well, I could tell from her writing style that had an underlying tone of worry in it. In the year we worked together, we had many heart-to-hearts, and I genuinely got the feeling she cared. She had no idea what I had been going through over the prior two weeks, but something clearly came through in my posts, even more so in our lengthy phone conversation that afternoon.

Perhaps, subconsciously, I was writing—and posting—as a desperate cry for help instead of a means to support and inspire others. Either way, I felt like I was finally starting to embrace who I really was.

24

FINDING MEDITATION

For the first time in years, I felt like I could take a deep breath.

By this point, we were about eighteen months into the COVID-19 pandemic, and our Oregon suburb was slowly starting to open up again. I could finally leave the house to do more than grocery shop. Every couple of days, I'd don a mask and lather up with hand sanitizer so I could make my way safely into the world. Weekday afternoons were reserved for the gym; on slow Saturday mornings, I wrote at my favorite local coffee shop; Matt and I resumed our dinner dates, opting to eat outside when the weather allowed for it—all things I desperately missed during quarantine. To top it off, my parents and brother visited for the first time in a year in a half. Getting back to my pre-pandemic routine reinvigorated me in more ways than one.

The therapist I'd been seeing encouraged me to take up meditation and mindfulness activities to support my healing journey and still my mind, something I desperately needed amidst the chaos of the world. I tried a handful of different apps he recommended, but it wasn't until I found ways to integrate meditation into my daily routine that I really started to see the benefits.

One part of my routine became the most prized moment of my day: making a coffee-shop style latte, which is ironic because I had a severe intolerance to caffeine. In an ideal world, I shouldn't have had anything with caffeine in it—not espresso, not tea, not kombucha, not chocolate. Not even decaf, which I learned in my days as a barista, still has caffeine, about 25 percent of the amount in a shot of espresso or regular cup of coffee. With even just a few bites of chocolate, my stomach swelled so much that it looked like I was six months pregnant. Within minutes, I felt nauseated, yet I ate it anyway. Some things, like mini chocolate chips in my cereal or a decaf latte, I just wasn't willing to give up.

In the hours before the rest of the world woke up, I'd pad down to my kitchen in my pajamas, eager to make a fancy drink. Much like how I had to adjust to the fifty mile-per-hour speed limit upon moving to Oregon, the process of pulling a shot of espresso with a delicate balance of richness and bitterness with no sour aftertaste forced me to slow down.

The process started with something so simple, preheating the espresso machine, but was often something I forget to do in so many areas of my life. I typically jumped into things headfirst without thought—starting workouts without stretching, putting oil into a cold skillet, jumping into a project with no preparation—and doing this simple act each morning reminded me to slow down, not only in my coffee routine, but in other areas of my life, too.

While the machine preheated, I took the opportunity to prepare, another step I often bypassed in everyday life. I wiped out the hardened grinds from the previous day's drink and gathered my tools: milk frother, espresso cup, distributor, calibrated tamp, scale and serving bowl or mug.

Once the machine warmed up, I pulled out my scale and got to work. I measured exactly 12.2 grams of whole beans and poured the weighed amount into the hopper. From there, I finely ground the beans using the machine's built-in grinder and a very methodical way of filling the portafilter so it didn't overflow. If I looked away during this moment and it overflowed, the ratio of coffee to water would be off when I pulled the shot. It was a domino effect that quite literally could make or break the final drink.

Once the grinds were safely and precisely piled into the portafilter, I used a distributor tool to, you guessed it, evenly distribute the grinds before tamping it. Distributing the coffee made sure that the grinds were evenly spread throughout the portafilter; if they weren't, I'd have an uneven extraction. Tamping, when I'd compress the grinds into a puck, was an extremely important step, making it so the water soaked up the flavor in the roasted beans before exiting the group head, rather than flowing straight through the grinds.

From there, I secured the portafilter in the group head, the heart of the machine, and got ready to pull a shot. This was where it got even more tricky because I measured the amount of espresso in grams and also time: how long the extraction takes, down to the second. Pulling 30.0 grams of espresso in twenty-five seconds, my ideal scenario, resulted in a golden-hued shot that was topped with a thick layer of honey-brown crema. It was magic, honestly.

At this point, I hadn't even thought about steaming the milk yet, and you can't have a coffee-shop-style latte without steamed milk and a layer of frothy foam. While my espresso machine had a steam wand, I preferred to use a stand-alone milk frother for ease and consistency.

As soon as the espresso was ready and the milk frothed, I worked quickly to pull the drink together. If I was feeling fancy, I'd add either store-bought or homemade syrup into the bowl before adding my espresso and finishing with the steamed milk. With the final masterpiece in hand, I took it to the couch or out to the patio, closed my eyes and enjoyed the first sip of bliss.

In the same way this morning routine kept me grounded throughout the difficult times, so did traditional meditation. For many years, I convinced myself I hated meditation. Maybe it was because I always envisioned meditation as that moment in *Eat, Pray, Love* where Liz sits down to meditate and almost instantly starts focusing on not swatting the fly on top of her nose instead of quieting her mind. When she opens her eyes after what feels like forever, it hasn't even been a minute.

Or maybe because I grew up thinking of meditation in a very stereotypical way. When someone asked me what meditation was, words like strict, silence, quiet, time-consuming, hippie and religion came to mind. I also wondered if it's because, when I started to seriously start thinking and learning about meditation, it was from my brother and mom, both of whom practiced Transcendental Meditation, a practice where they used a mantra to guide you through two twenty-minute sessions every day. The idea alone brought on a host of anxious thoughts:

Twenty minutes in complete silence? There's no possible way.

Is it even possible for me to sit still for twenty minutes straight?

Why do you need to pay a thousand dollars to learn how to meditate?

Is this a rip-off? A scam?

Is it really worth going to a four-day session to get a mantra and learn how to sit in silence?

Seriously, forty minutes a day? Who has the time?

One day, in dire need of a calm mind, I attempted to sit in silence. I sat down on the couch, set my timer for five minutes, and waited for the magic of meditation to happen, for my mind to completely clear. Instead, it started running a million miles a minute: *What if I didn't set my alarm? How much time is left? What's for dinner? Did I forget to take my medicine? I'm hungry. How long has it been? Am I allowed to pet the dog while sitting in silence? I wonder how the dog is doing. Does she love me? Is she happy? Oh, it's almost her dinner time, which means it's almost my dinner time, too. What's for dinner?*

I blinked my eyes open, struggling for the life of me to figure out how this was calming to some people. I looked at my phone; I had only been sitting still for two minutes. A whole 120 seconds, my mind nowhere near silence.

As someone who sprinted through life rather than walking, I kept coming back to meditation, even after my failed attempt. I tried a variety of different styles, from walking meditations to guided meditations to meditation apps. I tried to visualize my thoughts as clouds going by and cars driving past. I spent nights counting sheep and, a couple of times, tried a unique meditation where you hold your arms straight above your head for the entirety of Eminem's "Lose Yourself" five-minute-and-twenty-three-second song, which turned out to be more workout and less meditation.

In the spirit of Transcendental Meditation, I picked mantras to repeat to myself. I also counted my inhales and exhales and watched YouTube videos. Out of everything I tried, only one thing really stuck: a mantra-based YouTube video where I repeated the words, "I choose to let go" time and time again. After watching the same video over one hundred times, I got sick of it. Instead of feeling calm, I was bored. I kept looking for other meditations but just couldn't find one that resonated. Until I found Peloton.

To celebrate the new year, Peloton offered a sixty-day free trial. I signed up for the app, thinking I would get a good sweat on our knock-off indoor cycling setup. Little did I know their app offered so much more, including a meditation library with hundreds, if not thousands, of guided meditations ranging from five to thirty minutes.

I started small: a five-minute meditation class, the instructor's soothing voice keeping me company the entire time. The next day, I did a different five-minute meditation, followed by another one the third day. Over time, I explored breathing meditations, body scans, and emotion-based classes on top of calming and deep relaxation sessions.

Without a doubt, the meditations that made the biggest difference were sleep meditations. For many years, I convinced myself I was a good sleeper, telling myself that I got eight hours of sleep, regardless of where I was. After getting a Fitbit, I realized that wasn't the case at all. Sure, I'd be in bed for eight hours a night, but I only averaged six hours of sleep. The day I found sleep meditations was the day that my sleep schedule and my meditation practice both started falling into place.

For the first month or so, I tried a different sleep meditation every night. I tried different instructors and lengths, soon realizing that the twenty-minute practices were my sweet spot. And then, like magic, I found *the* sleep meditation. One night, I came upon a twenty-minute sleep meditation released earlier that day and clicked play, not thinking twice. For some reason, maybe the combination of the instructor's voice or the flow of the class, this particular meditation made me feel calmer than I did while lying in corpse pose at the end of a yoga practice. At the end of the day, my mind was typically a bundle of thoughts on a series of rollercoasters, but that night, my breath slowed, my heart rate went down, and, for what might have been the first time in my entire life, I was able to fall asleep without a bunch of thoughts trying to fight their way to the front of my brain.

For ninety days straight, I did that same sleep meditation every single night before bed. Interestingly, it also inspired me to meditate more often beyond sleep, too. On stressful days, I'd take five minutes in between calls to fit in a quick meditation, knowing that five minutes of deep breathing would lower my heart rate by as much as twenty beats per minute. I truly never thought I would enjoy meditation, but I did. I looked forward to hitting play and hearing the instructor's voice lure me to sleep. It became an essential part of my routine that I couldn't live without.

Until I found guided meditation, my practice came in the form of lap swimming. I came back to the water here and there over the years, at one point for competitive swimming in the form of triathlon, but it wasn't the same. In training, I'd work toward a set goal: to swim a short-distance, so I would only swim that distance and call it a day, often leaving the pool after only twenty or thirty minutes, before the meditative effects hit.

Before and during the COVID-19 pandemic, though, I found my way back to the pool in desperate need of a calm mind to balance the heaviness of the world. Although I was thoroughly out of shape, it felt like riding a bike, both the technique and the meditation coming back in no time. Once I made it through the warm-up, I'd tune out of the world and think solely in terms of the number of yards I was swimming.

Five hundred.

One thousand.

Three thousand.

Lap after lap, my mind cleared a little more. By the end of an hour of back-and-forths, the anxiety, depression, and work stress moved to the back of my mind and, instead, I'd notice the splash of water on my face as I turned my head to breathe; the power in my legs as I kicked off the wall; the rays of sunshine hitting my back.

Finding and prioritizing these moments of relaxation, whether in the form of making espresso, following a guided meditation, or swimming laps until my mind cleared became essential to my healing journey.

25

LESSONS FROM DAD

My right foot started tapping uncontrollably and I began to shake nonstop, nerves making their way to the surface. Instead of sitting patiently in the waiting room of my therapist's office, I was pacing back and forth, eager to share the realization I just had on the thirty-minute drive over. I arrived ten minutes early, which almost never happened.

As soon as my therapist opened the door and said goodbye to the patient before me, I jumped straight up and hustled into the room. Before I sat down, I said, "I had a revelation on the way over here," anxious to get this thought out of my head and into the real world.

"Let's hear it," he said.

By this point, we'd spent over fifteen hours in the same room and just barely skimmed the surface of my life, talking mostly about work and personal projects while avoiding harder topics, a subconscious way of keeping myself in a bubble to avoid discomfort of any kind. In fact, it wasn't until our last session that we started talking about something with any real substance to it.

It all started with a pillow.

When I walked into the room the prior week, I made a joke about how my biggest challenge is deciding which pillow to hold throughout our session. He's the type of therapist you see on TV shows who has dozens of pillows squashed onto the couch, and picking the coziest one is a game. Instead of the comment simply being brushed off, it led to a conversation about how I'm using the pillow as a physical barrier between the two of us.

He asked a seemingly easy question: "Are you afraid I'm going to judge you?"

I laughed it off, saying, "probably," and moved onto a different—safer—conversation. But as I really started to think about it, that was exactly it. Sure, I was being open and vulnerable and talking about what was happening in my life, but I did so with a filter. Even the conversations about my dark, suicidal thoughts were just barely touched upon, a part of me unwilling to scratch the still-healing scab, worried that it would scare him away. Like every other relationship in my life, I wanted him to like me.

But this conversation—that pillow—changed everything. It had been six days since I made that comment, and I quite literally hadn't stopped thinking about the damn pillow.

He's right, I realized. I was guarded—not just with him, but with everyone. I cared so much about what others thought; it was exhausting. I built this metaphorical wall, scared to subject myself to rejection. Instead of working to break the wall down, I spent my energy adding bricks to it, making it stronger and stronger as a way to keep myself holed up in the safety and comfort of my own thoughts, where I couldn't get hurt.

"I'm done having my guard up," I told him. "I'm exhausted and over it. We're doing this without the pillow today."

"*Fuck yeah,*" he responded, raising his fists in victory. It was time to get vulnerable.

We picked up where we left off the prior week: talking about my dad.

My dad is the most inspiring person I know. He's strong, driven, smart, and everything I admire in a person. He has overcome so much in his life—going from working at eight years old to support his family through extreme poverty to becoming a surgeon and, later, one of California's foremost worker's compensation experts. He is truly my hero, the person who I strive to grow into one day. So it's no surprise that, according to my therapist, I've subconsciously spent my whole life doing everything in my power to make him proud.

In reflecting on our conversation the prior week, I noticed about a hundred different ways how similar I am to my dad. Like him, my skin has an olive undertone and my eyes and hair are dark brown, erring on the verge of black. My eyebrows are bushy and full; in fact, they're my favorite feature of his that I inherited. We're both tall, muscular, and heavy-set. Beyond physical appearance, we're both extremely driven, competitive, and fiercely loyal to those we love. We bond over food, exercise, and learning in all forms. I get my love of working, cooking, eating, and, to his dismay, cracking my knuckles from him. When I talk, I unknowingly use "you know" as my go-to filler word over "um" or "ah," just like he does. Even my car is perpetually messy like his.

My dad is the first person I call when I'm sick. Although I had a family care doctor growing up, I never trusted her the way I trusted my dad. When something was wrong, I'd walk him through a detailed list of symptoms and he'd diagnose me either in person or over the phone. I trust my dad with my life.

Weight was also a constant conversation for us. Each time we talked, we discussed what foods we're making, avoiding, and indulging in. We shared the workouts we were doing and feigned frustration when we noticed the scale barely budging or celebrated when it moved a lot. We set weight loss goals and resolutions together, sticking to some but mostly choosing to try something new every few months or so. I suppose you could say bonding over weight loss—or lack thereof—has been our thing for... ever.

As I explained all of this to my therapist, I stopped mid-sentence.

Holy shit, I thought. *I know the root cause of my struggle around weight. It's not the thyroid issues or the bullying or my inner critic; it's the relationship with my dad. If everything I do is to connect with and relate to him, of course I'm going to hesitate to give up something we bond over.*

I asked myself a series of hypothetical questions: If I end up losing weight, will our relationship suffer if we don't have goals or diets to bond over? If I choose to let go of talking about weight loss, would we find something new to discuss? Would I still make him proud?

I said all of this out loud to the therapist, and he had the same reaction I did: mind. blown.

He put a fist on each side of his head and made a *pow* sound while widening his hands, showing how his brain, like mine, exploded at the revelation.

As therapists do, he believes your childhood heavily influences who you are today. While it doesn't predict how you'll live or act, what you learned growing up influences how you think about your self-worth, relationships, safety, and many other things. Particularly for those who have experienced some level of trauma, which I had, the impact of said challenges can follow someone into adulthood, showing up in ways such as shame, guilt, depression, heightened anxiety, low self-esteem, and distorted memories or perspectives.

So, of course, it makes sense that this relationship is at the heart of one of my biggest internal struggles. Of *course*. I honestly don't know how I didn't think about it until that moment.

By the time I put two and two together, we reached our allotted fifty minutes together. I drove home in silence instead of listening to a top forty hit on repeat like I normally would. As I inched forward in rush hour traffic, my mind wandered, recalling moments from my childhood that I had previously repressed.

My dad washing my mouth out with soap when I said a bad word.

My dad stopping the car at the bottom of our very steep hill, yelling at me to get out and start walking, then inching beside me in the car as I walked the 0.8 miles home in tears—all because I made a snide comment about my mom.

My dad pushing me flush against the wall, grabbing my neck and forcing me to "stand straight; don't slouch" when I got in trouble.

As soon as I got home, I grabbed my computer and rushed to the couch, eager to pull up my Notes app so I could reflect on these memories until I could talk through them at the following week's therapy session.

I wrote down some of the key lessons I learned while growing up: I was taught to stand tall when things were falling apart and push my emotions as far down as they could possibly go. I learned to put my head down and do whatever it takes to accomplish something. I learned to respect those around me, put others before myself, and follow through with my responsibilities and commitments, no matter what.

As I was typing all of this out, I googled, "traits army parents teach kids" wondering if these were influenced, perhaps, by my dad's time in the armed forces. I wasn't at all prepared for what I came across: LDRSHIP, an acronym for the basic values of the United States Army, that come together to form the seven key principles that soldiers learn in detail during Basic Combat Training:

- **Loyalty:** Bear true faith and allegiance to the US Constitution, the Army, your unit and other soldiers.
- **Duty:** Fulfill your obligations.
- **Respect:** Treat people as they should be treated.
- **Selfless Service:** Put the welfare of the nation, the Army, and your subordinates before your own.
- **Honor:** Live up to all the Army values.
- **Integrity:** Do what's right, legally and morally.
- **Personal Courage:** Face fear, danger, or adversity [physically or morally].

Soldiers are expected to live these values every day, in everything they do, whether they're on the job or off.

I sat there in awe, connecting dots that had been floating randomly around my mind for nearly thirty years.

These principles, when applied to modern parenting, embodied the lessons I learned growing up and continue to live by today.

As I clicked around the official US Army site, I saw a small link on the left-hand side of the page leading to something called the Soldier's Creed. Out of curiosity, I opened the page and almost dropped my jaw as I read the short but powerful statement:

I am an American Soldier.
I am a warrior and a member of a team.
I serve the people of the United States, and live the Army Values.
I will always place the mission first.
I will never accept defeat.
I will never quit.
I will never leave a fallen comrade.
I am disciplined, physically and mentally tough, trained and proficient in my warrior tasks and drills.
I always maintain my arms, my equipment, and myself.
I am an expert and I am a professional.
I stand ready to deploy, engage, and destroy the enemies of the United States of America in close combat.
I am a guardian of freedom and the American way of life.
I am an American Soldier.

I know little about my dad's time in the Army. He didn't like to talk about it, and I never wanted to force him to open old wounds, so I never asked about his time in the service. Reading these two army standards, the

LDRSHIP values and the Soldier's Creed, taught me so much about him that I had never considered before.

Of *course* he taught me to be loyal, disciplined, and professional in every situation; it's what he was taught to do. While I saw some of his tactics as strict, he was merely instilling a sense of character in me and my brother, at least according to the Army. He led by example, teaching us to become the kind of upstanding citizen he was taught to be. He was simply handing down the lessons he learned to us. He was doing the best he could—as a parent *and* as a soldier.

As I reflected on all of this, I realized that he's an even better man than I've ever given him credit for. I'm immensely grateful for all the lessons he taught me, even if I felt like they were sometimes taken a bit too far. Because of him, I stand by my loved ones through thick and thin, no questions asked. In any situation, I inherently do what's morally right, even if it's hard or uncomfortable. When I wholeheartedly commit to something or someone, I do everything possible to follow through and complete the task at hand. I treat others with dignity, respect, and honor and put others before myself—not because I'm not worth it, but because that's the type of person my dad is.

Feeling at peace about myself and our relationship for the first time in years, I gave myself permission to finally let this piece of me go. I know without a doubt that we'll find other things to talk about and bond over beyond something as trivial as weight loss.

I'm my father's daughter; that in itself means so much more than any number on the scale.

CONCLUSION

Thursday, October 11, 2021. 7:14 a.m.

I slowly opened my eyes, adjusting to the morning light peeking in between the blinds. As I stretched, I took a deep breath and resettled my mind, recalling the dream I just had.

My brother went on a rampage, killing anyone who crossed his path. After unsuccessfully hiding in plain sight, I was shot, blood covering my white shirt as the bullet grazed my stomach. Frozen in place and terrified to move, I started thinking of my next move; where I could go to feel safe. Instead of going home to my husband for support and solace, I went straight to my ex-boyfriend. Unlike some of my other dreams, our relationship mirrored the one we had in real life: we broke up many years before but kept in touch here and there until we didn't. Also like reality, our relationship in the dream was a tug-of-war of who came running back to the other first. This time, I was begging for his attention, using "I was just shot" as an excuse to pull him away from his girlfriend and into my arms instead.

As always, I woke up before seeing how the dream ended.

When I started taking the antidepressants, I wasn't aware the vivid dreams would become a regular occurrence. My dreams, often frightening and unsettling, were so real. It was like *Inception* come to life; I knew I was safe at home, in bed, but I woke up drenched in sweat, able to recall every movement, action, and spoken word perfectly, like I was there. Experiencing intense dreams each night was a small sacrifice to make to feel more like myself during the day.

Another constant in my routine was something I dreaded for years. Each morning, I'd shuffle over to the scale and squeeze my eyes as I waited for my weight to flash on the screen. If the number went down, I told myself it would be a good day. If it stayed the same or went up, I cursed myself like no other, falling deeper into a hole of self-depreciation. This morning, I stepped on the scale and waited patiently as my weight processed. When the number came up, I simply made a mental note and let it go. It was a data point and nothing more. Like the size on the back of the jeans that no longer fit, it's just a number, not a way to make or ruin my day.

From there, I went down to the kitchen for my favorite part of the day—coffee. Except for the fact I was no longer drinking caffeine. I was on day three of trying out a new adaptogenic coffee alternative instead of my beloved freshly ground, locally roasted decaf espresso beans. Although the smell and taste couldn't begin to compare, giving up my morning latte was easier than I anticipated. Within twenty minutes of finishing my herbal sugar-free caramel soy cappuccino, there was no stitch in my side, and the anxiety I typically felt within an hour of sipping a latte was nonexistent. I made a mental note to try it again tomorrow, confident I'd get used to the earthy taste sooner rather than later.

Once I finished my warm drink, I cozied up on the couch, iPad in hand. When COVID-19 first hit, the first thing I did upon waking—before coffee, before anything—was check the case count and death toll. Every thirty minutes thereafter, I'd refresh *The New York Times* homepage, eager to see what had changed. Senseless murders, bomb threats, and coronavirus updates overtook my mind from the second I woke up to the second I went to bed. To help manage my heightened anxiety, I bought a digital subscription to *The Oregonian*, my local newspaper, to eliminate the need to follow online news sources. I now got the news in one fell swoop each morning, allowing me to feel up to date without being tied to my phone, a modern-day digital leash. I skimmed each headline, making a point to read *On This Day in History* and the various advice columns before settling in to do the WONDERWORD, a word search within a word search, and the daily Jumble, a word puzzle I grew up doing with my mom and brother each Sunday morning over breakfast. Instead of starting my day immersed in other people's lives on social media, I woke up to word puzzles. *Much* better.

After solving both puzzles and reading the comics, I meandered upstairs to get ready for the day. I stripped down and headed into the bathroom for a shower, staring at my reflection as I waited for the water to heat up. Three years ago, I made a pact with myself to stop wearing makeup and start taking better care of my skin as a way of embracing who I am—freckles, melasma, excessive weight and all. As I looked at the woman in front of me, I saw some things, like my sagging belly lined with stretch marks, that bothered me, but I didn't let them bring me down as I once did. I met my eyes in the mirror, zoning in on my face. Instead of classifying my pimples, blemishes, and bushy eyebrows as imperfections, I saw them as something that makes me... me. They defined who I was, right in that moment.

You have made it through so much, I silently told the woman looking back at me, applauding her for coming so far in the last few years.

Later that morning, I called my dad to say hi. We had been talking on a near-daily basis, our relationship evolving more than it ever had once I started opening up to him about my mental health struggles.

"Lauren Shaber," he boomed, answering the phone as he always did. It didn't matter that I legally changed my name to Lauren Bartleson; I'd always have his last name.

"Hi, Dad," I responded. "Just calling to say hi."

"I love when you call. What are you up to today, sweetheart?"

"Not much, just working. I might try to go to the pool later to get in a swim. What are you up to?"

Our conversations, which were once five minutes max, often lasted forty-five minutes or more. We'd go from talking about what history book he was reading to how our tomatoes and herbs were growing to what we were making for dinner. We exchanged recipes, bought the same cookbooks, and, every so often, planned to make the same dish on the same night so we could enjoy a meal together, despite being over seven hundred miles apart. He started opening up more about his childhood, telling me stories that I hadn't heard before. We talked about what was going on at work, what upgrades he was doing around the house, and what errands we each had to run that day. Whether we were talking about everything or nothing, these conversations became a highlight of my day.

"Are we still on for Sunday?" he asked. "6:30?"

"Wouldn't miss it," I replied. For years, my dad talked about doing a weekly family dinner, but being spread throughout two, sometimes, three states or continents, it wasn't feasible... until Zoom. When the COVID-19 pandemic hit, my family joined a meeting from our respective houses for a Shabbat dinner one Friday night. Although we were all small faces on a screen, it felt like we were all sitting around a table together, laughing and talking over each other like we normally would. We stayed online for two hours, well after our plates were cleared and dessert was served. We logged in the next Friday, and then the next, and then the next. Over time, we shifted from Fridays to Sundays, but our weekly gathering became tradition. I looked forward to it each week.

"Okay, kiddo, I'll let you go," he said. "I'm going to get back to work. Who loves you?"

"You."

"How long for?"

"Always."

I hung up with a smile on my face, already thinking of something I wanted to tell him the next time we talked. There was never enough time.

A few hours later, I absentmindedly picked up my phone and opened the Instagram app. After an eighteen-month hiatus, I recently started posting again. The difference between then and now? This time around, I wasn't hiding. Behind each photo was a caption with real talk rather than a perfectly designed and edited description made to look like I had it all together.

I thought back to a notification I received a few days prior. A stranger left a comment on one of my posts telling me that she, too, had a broken brain for thirty-five years and applauded me, encouraging me to keep up the great work. As soon as I read her comment, my mind started running in circles, thinking about how I could tell her "thanks but no thanks" for the backhanded compliment.

Instead of pouncing and letting my anger go wild in my reply, I simply let it go for the time being, vowing to come back to it when my mind was clear. I would much rather take the time to respond kindly than lash out in frustration, whether it took two minutes, two hours, or two days for my emotions to settle. Just because life on the internet moves at the speed of light doesn't mean I have to.

It had been three days, and I was ready to respond with honesty and kindness. I replied, "I'm not sure I love the term 'broken brain,' but I understand what you're saying and am proud of you for taking care of yourself. Thank you for your support."

It was true. I did understand what she's saying. My therapist explained to me that depression results from a complicated chemical imbalance. Too much or too little of a certain chemical didn't simply cause a shift in my mood and how I experienced life. A combination of millions, maybe even billions, of chemical reactions paired with genetics, stress, medication, medical challenges, and environmental factors made me feel the way I did when I was in a "funk." With that said, I didn't think my brain was broken. Just because I needed to give my brain a little extra love in the form of medication didn't make me less than someone who didn't experience symptoms of depression.

In addition to taking my daily medications, I was trying to do a better job of taking care of myself by eating well and moving regularly. Despite my loud and obnoxious "I hate diets" rants in my head and online, I finally gave in—a little. I hadn't touched gluten since the endocrinologist told me to avoid it, and I was more aware of what I put into my body. I wanted to live a life that I was proud of; one that brought me joy. A big part of that was eating meals that taste good but also make me *feel* good.

That same day, I had a steak salad with chips and queso from Chipotle. Matt and I sat next to each other at the kitchen table, catching up on our mornings, as we ate. Despite both working from home, it was the first time we'd seen each other all day.

"I had another dream," I told him, unable to look him in the eyes, the guilt holding tightly.

"About your ex?" he asked in between bites of his own chicken salad.

"Yeah," I mumbled, immediately going for another bite. I hoped he didn't ask what the dream was about; I hated reliving my all-too-real dreams, giving my ex more mindshare than he deserved.

Matt didn't ask. Instead, he said with a sad smile, "I wish you dreamt about me every night."

"Me too, love." I sighed. "Me too."

"Maybe tonight's the night," he said with a grin and a shoulder bump, instantly pushing the awkwardness aside.

"I sure hope so."

Another big part of my daily routine was prioritizing movement, even on the days that I didn't want to exercise. After years away from the water, I recently found my way back to the pool and swam one or two miles, often over one hundred laps, a few times a week. While I loved being able to tell my app that I burned over seven hundred calories in a workout, it was more than that. I swam until the swirling thoughts of *shoulda, coulda, woulda* settled down and all that remained was the number of yards I'd swum so far. Sometimes it took twenty minutes for my mind to clear and other times it took seventy-five, but it didn't matter. By the time I pulled myself out of the water, showered, and drove home, I was tired in the best sense. For a few minutes, my always-present anxiety was hidden, too exhausted to show its face.

Sometimes, I found the energy to do a spin class or toning workout after or instead of a swim. When inspiration struck, like it did that night, I headed downstairs to our dimly lit basement to do one of my favorite ten-minute toning workouts from the program I scolded for so many years. In the video's intro, I saw two women dancing around on the beach, laughing, and having fun. For so long, all I felt when I watched that thirty-second clip was jealously of their perfect life; now, I could only envision how much prep work went into making this the perfect production: high-quality cameras, lighting, editing, a strict twelve-hundred-calorie diet for months in advance, hair, makeup, lighting, and more. Life on social media isn't always what it seems. I know that now.

As I had this epiphany, I thought about what I had put my husband through in the height of my social media obsession. Each night after making dinner, I'd say, "I just need to take a quick photo for Instagram." I'd spend a good five to ten minutes styling each plate, doing my best to replicate layouts from other famous food bloggers. Once I was happy with the food styling, I moved onto styling the props. I'd gather napkins, cutlery, and anything else I felt was necessary to create the "perfect" photo. When it was just right, I'd set up my indoor lighting stand and place reflectors exactly where they needed to be. I'd grab my fancy camera and take some tester images, adjusting the plate, props, and reflectors as necessary. Once I landed on the perfect layout and adjusted the settings on my camera, I'd take no less than one hundred photos.

Twenty or thirty minutes after serving, our plates and food cold, we could finally eat. Because our dining room table was overtaken with photography gear, we made our way to the couch. Immediately after scarfing down my meal, I'd pick up my phone, transferring the photos from the app to my phone and jumping straight into editing: cropping, straightening, and white balance in one app, and filters, clarity, contrast, brightness, saturation, vibrancy, temperature, shadows, exposure, and sharpening in another. If I wanted the photo on a white background, I'd have to bring up a third app. Once the photo was *just right*, I opened the Notes app to start drafting my caption. At the end of each post, I listed a few hashtags, which enabled me to interact with others in the community. When all was said and done, often over an hour later, I could finally hit post. As soon as I did, I started interacting with others on the platform, getting lost in consuming, liking, and commenting on their content. Before I knew it, two hours had gone by. I'd look up, confused not to see Matt. Despite being in the same room, I was in a completely different world, so much so that I didn't see him leave or hear him say goodbye.

Why did I let social media—and everything else—get in the way of my relationship, the thing that matters most? I scolded myself.

Rather than feeling angry, I felt sad. Sad that I'd let this version of me—the one that was obsessed with likes and comments and follows—pull me away from something, *someone*, so special. Someone who had put up with so much over the years, doing nothing but supporting and cheering me on along the way. My husband woke up early to be at the races so he would be the first person I saw when I crossed the finish line. He asked the waiter what gluten free options they had, just in case I forgot. He listened when I rambled through my muddled thoughts, hugged me when I was down, and took care of me when I needed him, and even when I didn't. I knew I was fortunate to have such a strong built-in support system in my parents and brother, but until that moment, I genuinely didn't realize how lucky I truly was to have such an amazing partner.

Before heading to bed, I walked into his office to both apologize to and thank him.

"Hey, love," I said as I knocked twice on his door.

He pulled off his headphones and smiled over at me. "Hi, lovebug. What's up?"

"Can you talk for a second? I wanted to tell you something."

"Of course," he said, standing and meeting me halfway for a hug.

"I was just working out and was thinking about me and you."

"Oh, no." He laughed. When I said something like that, it was usually followed by something big or small that I wanted to fix in our relationship.

"It's not bad," I promised.

I wasn't sure how to sum up my thoughts, so I simply said, "I know I've put you through a lot these past few years," as I wrapped my arms around his waist. "It's been a wild ride. Thank you for loving me through it all."

EPILOGUE

To be totally honest, I don't know how my story will end.

In between writing about overcoming bullying, grief, and trauma while relocating, falling in love, and figuring out who I am both online and off, I've wondered countless times what the ending would be. Multiple times throughout the process I went to my husband, giddy and excited to tell him, "I just thought of my conclusion!" Each time I wrote it, though, it felt too perfect for a book like this.

I've been trained to look for happy endings—in books, in relationships, in life. In writing this book, however, I realized that's not who I am. As much as I hate to admit it, I'm not an optimistic person. I'm flawed and imperfect and worry too much about what other people think. In a book titled *Behind the Facade*, I can't write a promise of anything, much less something that isn't totally and unequivocally me.

The hard truth is that I don't know what the next minute, hour, day, or decade will bring. What I've learned with depression and anxiety is that things can change in the blink of an eye. I can be in the middle of a good day, and then, as fast as a light switches on, my mood changes. Maybe a panic attack washes over me and I struggle to breathe through it. Maybe exhaustion hits and I just *can't* anymore. Maybe suicidal thoughts creep in and take over, pulling me into a dark abyss that wasn't there five seconds ago.

Anxiety and depression are not a one-size-fits-all experience. Heck, life isn't one-size-fits-all. I spent many years hiding from the world, pretending to be what I thought other people wanted me to be, when in reality, I was just hiding from myself.

Writing this book allowed me to look back on the moments I've been holding on to for so long, afraid to loosen my grip on, much less fully let go of. It's scary to put your truth out there; to break out of the curated feeds and perfectly edited photos and say, "Hey, I'm human, and I have no freaking clue what I'm doing," but here I am, putting my truth out there for the world to see.

This is the real me.

FINAL THOUGHTS

My drawn-out journey to autoimmune and mental diagnoses wasn't unique. According to the National Institutes of Health (NIH), between 14.7 and 23.5 million Americans (8 percent of the population) have an autoimmune disease. The average time for an autoimmune diagnosis is 4.6 years, and during that period, the patient typically sees 4.8 doctors, according to the American Autoimmune Related Diseases Association (AARDA). The connection between autoimmune diseases and mental health disorders is also important to note. A 2016 study of one hundred patients with hypothyroidism found that 60 percent reported some degree of depression, while 63 percent showed some degree of anxiety.

I am extremely grateful to have received the diagnoses and treatment that I have. I don't take the privilege of having insurance, the ability to take time away from work for appointments, and access to doctors, mental health professionals, and medication for granted.

Thank you to the amazing doctors, nurses, and health care workers who listen to patient concerns and work tirelessly to find a diagnosis. It goes a long way for a patient to feel seen and heard. An extra special thank you for putting your lives on line during the COVID-19 pandemic. You are all heroes.

ACKNOWLEDGEMENTS

This story is so much more than one girl's healing journey.

If I've learned anything from the ups and downs we just relived together, it's that we are not alone in this life. While I wrote this book as a form of healing for myself, I chose to publish in hopes that it starts open and honest conversations about mental health. To those who have shared their stories and struggles with me in person or online, thank you. I appreciate it more than you know.

Thank you to Lee MacMillan and her friends and family who are continuing her mental health advocacy efforts. While I didn't know Lee personally, a piece of me will always feel connected to her. I hope Lee realized how much she inspired a movement, giving young people encouragement and permission to speak up about mental health. Selfishly, I wish I had the chance to meet Lee in person because I feel like we would have had an instant connection, but I'm grateful beyond belief to have had the opportunity to get to know her online. This is why I love the internet so much; not for the grief that comes with losing someone who feels like a friend or the hate comments or the trolls, but the opportunity to get to "meet" and know someone who you would have otherwise never had the opportunity to connect with. I will continue to #speakupforlee in hopes that I can be the friend to someone else that Lee was to me in my darkest moments.

A special thank you to Andie Mitchell, whose book, *It Was Me All Along*, moved with me from desk to couch to wherever I was writing as inspiration for what this story could turn into one day.

Thank you to the following musicians and bands whose music came together to create the nineteen-song playlist that got me through my lowest points: By the Coast, Griffin, SLANDER, Callie Lehman, Duncan Laurence, Imagine Dragons, Cyril Hahn, Kotomi, One Hundred Years, First Aid Kit, Halcyon, Valentina Franco, The Light the Heat, LEISURE, Parcels, Alex Metric, Matt Simons, Damien Jurado, filious, Alicia Keys, Patricia van Haastrecht, Prince of Spain, and Austin Mackay. Your music saved and comforted me in a way I'll never be able to express.

Thank you to each and every person who contributed funds to help bring this book to life:

Alan Goldstein
Alexa Hayon
Ali Miller
Alison Cartier
Allyson Davies
Alyssa Semerdjian
Alyx Kay
Amanda Bender
Amanda Bidmon
Amelia Elisa Villarreal

Amy Banocy
Angela Bartleson
Ankit Thakkar
Anuj Baveja
Ashish Shah
Ashley Grosfeld
Ashley Groves
Ashraf Seddeek
Avalon Bauman
Bailee Noella

Barbara & Paul Jaffe
Brady A Plevac
Bridget C Bisnette
Carlo Mahfouz
Carmen Maria Navarro
Carriann Ashcraft
Casey Kelby
Cate Cannon
Charlotte McCormack
Christine and Mark
	Mohammadpour
Christopher Pierce
Cornelia Pool
Cristina Lau
Cyndee Milligan
Cyndi Davis
Dan Zhu
Danielle Bostrom
Danielle Maschmeyer
Dasom Lee
Deborah Schenker
Diana Lane
Donica Merhazion
Eduardo Siu
Elena Gerstmann
Eli Mendoza
Elizabeth Hite
Emma Colvin
Eric Koester
Ericka Engelman
Erin OCallaghan
Fred Bartleson

Graciela Penso
Greg Avakian
Greg Gardner
Haley Newlin
Hayden Ogden
Alex Ilitchev
James King
Jennifer C Welsh
Jennifer Field
Jennifer Tam
Jeremy Schoales
Jeremy Teitelbaum
John Randall Pratt
John Thompson
Jon Simmonds
Josh Benavente
Josh Mork
Julia McCann
Justin Shaber
Karen Bartleson
Kat Kobe
Kathy Baird
Kathy Gill
Katy Weller
Katya Davydova
Kelley Riley
Kendall Rookey
Kristen Nguyen
Laura Hollencamp
Laura Nishimura
Lauren Aylott
Lauren DiTullio

Leah Lavery
Leslie Whigham
Lewis Choi
Lisa DeAngelis
Lisa Efstratis
Lisa Clark
Loren Lay
Lori Silver and Syd Shaber
Lorraine Nolan
Lynne Silver
Mackenzie Larson
Madeline Hatlen
Margaret Quintanilla
Mark Anderson
Mark Bartleson
Mark Stinson
Marlo Milligan Sharp
Matt Bartleson
Melanie Elizabeth Pitnick
Michael Radlove
Michelle McGovern
Morgan Graham
Nancy Allahan
Neha Shukla
Nina Jasper
Nirav Sheth
Petra Roth

Phil Vella
Pratyusha Mantha
Rachel Foxworthy
Rachel Wylie
Rebecca Garner
Rocio Del Carmen Lopez
Sabrina Thorp
Sally Etheridge
Samantha Johnson
Sandra Gonzalez
Sara Blasing
Sarah McGann
Sarah Sennett
Sarah Thomas
Sean Armstrong
Serge Friolet
Shannon Quist
Shayla Malek
Shirley Newson
Stacey Lee Coonrod
Susan Wise
Taylor Altfeld
Taylor Goodson
Taylor Morrison
Timothy Cheng
Tracy Baldwin
Victoria Wilson

You believed in this book when it was just a scrappy manuscript, and I'm beyond appreciative that you took a chance on me and this story. I hope it makes you proud.

To the team at New Degree Press: Thank you for making this book the absolute best it could be. A special thank you to Shanna Heath and Bianca Myrtil for your editing magic. This book wouldn't be what it is today without you.

Thank you to my amazing beta readers: Matthew Bartleson, Lori Silver, Syd Shaber, Karen Bartleson, and Barbara Jaffe. I appreciate each of you taking the time to read the drafts and provide early feedback. I couldn't have done it without you.

To my therapist: Thank you for letting me remove the pillow, lie on the floor, and open up on my own time and terms. You've shown me the value of looking inward, pushing forward, and giving myself grace. I genuinely look forward to our weekly session, regardless of whether we're talking sports or digging deep into childhood trauma. I appreciate your support, encouragement, and honesty—even when you challenge me.

I can't even begin to thank my family—not just for their support with this book, but for everything in life. The following is such a small snippet of the love I feel for each of you; take it with a grain of salt, a big hug, and a teary "I love you." Here we go.

To my amazing husband, Matt: I couldn't ask for a better partner in this life. As I write this, we're going on nine years together. Despite the rollercoaster we've been on, they've truly been the best years of my life, thanks to you. You are the kindest, most generous person I've ever met, and I genuinely can't wait to see what our future holds. I love you more than you will ever know.

Justin: You were the first person to ever tell me that you had the space to hold the weight I couldn't bear to hold, and I will never, ever take that offer for granted. You are the best brother a girl could ever ask for, and I am so thankful to have you in my life. No matter where you are in the world, I am just a call, drive, or flight away. I love you.

Mom: I don't even know where to start, so I'll just say you are the best mom in the world. You have no idea how special it is to be your daughter. Thank you for everything. I love you.

Dad, I said it in the dedication and I'll say it again here: You are my hero. How long for? Always.

Last, to you, the reader: Thank you for taking the time to read my work. There are hundreds of millions of books in this world, and I'm honored that you took the time to read mine. I don't take it for granted one bit. Thank you, thank you, thank you.

Additional
Materials

MENTAL HEALTH RESOURCES

Psychology Today

www.psychologytoday.com

Reaching out to a therapist was one of the hardest yet most rewarding things I've ever done. I found mine through Psychology Today, an online directory of clinical professionals, psychiatrists, and other specialists who provide mental health services. The filtering is easy to use. (Learn from my mistake and make sure to double-check you selected your insurance!) But more importantly, I felt comfortable messaging professionals via the confidential form on the site.

Therapy Den

www.therapyden.com

In the weeks after my downward spiral when I wasn't able to get access to a therapist, I tried Therapy Den, which I loved. The site is easy to navigate and feels very welcoming. While I didn't find a long-term fit, this site made me excited to go back to therapy. Through this site, I also found counselors who offer group hiking therapy, painting therapy, writing therapy, and other creative avenues to express your emotions.

Better Help
www.betterhelp.com

During that same time, I tried a service called Better Help at a friend's suggestion. Better Help offers online therapy so anyone who struggles with life's challenges can get help, anytime and anywhere. You can connect with a certified therapist within forty-eight hours. The service was more expensive than I thought, but I loved the convenience of being able to dial in from the couch, bed, or wherever I happened to be. You can also text with your therapist between appointments. It's a great service that I'd definitely consider using if I hadn't secured local support.

NAMI
www.nami.org

NAMI is the National Alliance on Mental Illness, the nation's largest grassroots mental health organization. I found out about NAMI after I went back to therapy for the second time, and, frankly, I wish I'd come across it sooner. In addition to a myriad of other offerings, my local chapter, NAMI Washington County, offers a full calendar of peer-run support groups for specific needs and families that would have been highly beneficial for when I couldn't have accessed a professional. There are more than six hundred state organizations across the United States, many of which offer similar support and education programs.

COMETRY

www.cometry.org

COMETRY is an art form that blends performance poetry and stand-up comedy into clean and clever entertainment. I attended their E.M.O.J.I. program through work and was blown away at how involved and emotional I was through Zoom. It was the first time that I heard topics like depression, anxiety, and suicide talked about in such a relatable, public way, and was by far one of the most powerful presentations I have ever seen. Iggy and Andre, the founders of COMETRY and the presenters of the E.M.O.J.I session I attended, are both outstanding artists, and I hope everyone gets a chance to see them perform at least once in their life.

Waking Up

www.wakingup.com

I've tried a lot of meditation apps over the years, and Waking Up is the one I keep coming back to for my daily practice. Sam's voice is really soothing, and he not only guides you during meditation but explains why you're doing what you're doing. For example, through one of my first few classes he guided me to listen to the sounds around me. I heard birds chirping, dogs barking, a plane flying above our house, and my husband walking around downstairs. He explained that I can't control any of those sounds. The dog will bark whether I want it to or not. A bird will chirp regardless of whether I give it permission. This was a turning point in my meditation journey, and something I hadn't learned through the other apps.

Peloton
www.onepeloton.com

Peloton is known for their indoor cycling bikes, but they have an app that offers so much more. As of writing, I use a DIY setup, where I place an iPad on the holder of a Schwinn bike. The bike we have records cadence but not resistance. I also connect a heart rate monitor so I can track my Strive score. I love this setup because it encourages me to listen to my body rather than pushing to meet or exceed the resistance recommended by the instructor. When I need to get deep in my feelings, I go straight for one of Christine's Reflection Rides; they're like therapy on the bike. Beyond cycling classes, I love Chelsea's sleep meditations. I also wholeheartedly recommend Aditi and Denis's restorative yoga classes, Emma's core classes, and Emma and Hannah C.'s stretching classes.

THE PLAYLIST: FOR LEE. FOR ME.

Much like writing, music is a form of therapy for me. I often listen to a song dozens, if not hundreds, of times on repeat until I've memorized every aspect—from the lyrics to the beat and how my body feels with each subtle change. Like a good book, music tells a story. Similar to how the characters come alive in a new-to-me novel or memoir, songs bring my emotions out in ways nothing else can. This playlist, named in honor of Lee MacMillan, is the one I listened to on repeat during my darkest times and is what I put on repeat when I'm feeling lost, lonely, or overwhelmed.

1. "I'll Get You Home" – By The Coast
2. "All You Need To Know (feat. Calle Lehmann)" – Gryffin, SLANDER, Calle Lehmann
3. "Arcade" – Duncan Laurence
4. "Walking The Wire" – Imagine Dragons
5. "Grace" – Cyril Hahn, Kotomi
6. "Reborn" – One Hundred Years
7. "Come Give Me Love" – First Aid Kit

8. "Runaway" – Halcyon, Valentina Franco
9. "Steady" – The Light the Heat
10. "It's Our Time" – The Light the Heat
11. "Slipping Away" – LEISURE
12. "Lightenup—Alex Metric Remix" – Parcels, Alex Metric
13. "Catch & Release—Deepend Remix" – Matt Simons, Deepend
14. "Ohio—filous Remix" – Damien Jurado, filous
15. "Good Job" – Alicia Keys
16. "Rainbow" – Patricia van Haastrecht
17. "Wild" – Prince of Spain
18. "Without You" – Austin Mackay
19. "Brighter Days" – The Light the Heat

APPENDIX

5 | Racing from Coast to Coast

Federal Bureau of Investigation. "Alcatraz Escape." *Famous Cases & Criminals*. Accessed May 2022. https://www.fbi.gov/history/famous-cases/alcatraz-escape.

8 | Hello, Haters

Anonymous. "Anyone follow laurenliveshealthy? She sort of irks me but I can't pinpoint why." *GOMI Blog,* August 17, 2015. https://gomiblog.com/forums/healthy-living-bloggers/fitness-igers/page-86/.

Anonymous. "http://www.laurenliveshealthy.com is my new fluff reversperation/hate read. Overall she's fairly harmless, just kind of dumb..." *GOMI Blog,* June 30, 2015. https://gomiblog.com/forums/healthy-living-bloggers/fitness-igers/page-86/.

Women's Health. "You go, Lauren!" *Facebook.* September 7, 2015. https://www.facebook.com/womenshealthmagazine/posts/10153558843401788.

9 | The Trolls Are Back

Anonymous. "I need this thread to happen. Especially now that she thinks she's important enough to post a whole thing about how she's #standinguptobullies..." *GOMI Blog,* April 20, 2017. https://gomiblog.com/forums/healthy-living-bloggers/wandering-in-wellnesslauren-lives-healthy/.

Anonymous. "I'm here and ready to make this thread happen! LLH is my favorite hate read. Her rant about GOMI just made me want to talk about her even more." *GOMI Blog,* April 20, 2017. https://gomiblog.com/forums/healthy-living-bloggers/wandering-in-wellnesslauren-lives-healthy/.

Anonymous. "Lauren posted an IG story rant about how she is staying off IG all weekend because she is comparing herself to other..." *GOMI Blog,* April 29, 2017. https://gomiblog.com/forums/healthy-living-bloggers/wandering-in-wellnesslauren-lives-healthy/.

Anonymous. "Omg smells like a mustard freak—almost spit out my water lmao..." *GOMI Blog,* May 1, 2017. https://gomiblog.com/forums/healthy-living-bloggers/wandering-in-wellnesslauren-lives-healthy/.

Anonymous. "So here's a post from earlier this year that I found to be just kind of laughable and what I think sets WiW apart from your average HLB..." *GOMI Blog,* April 12, 2017. https://gomiblog.com/forums/healthy-living-bloggers/wandering-in-wellnesslauren-lives-healthy/.

Anonymous. "The whole book thing strikes me as ridiculous. First of all, I wouldn't feel comfortable at all giving my money to someone..." *GOMI Blog,* April 22, 2017. https://gomiblog.com/forums/healthy-living-bloggers/wandering-in-wellnesslauren-lives-healthy/.

peanbuttfing [pseud.]."Does anyone here follow Lauren Lives Healthy (now Wandering In Wellness rolleyes)?" *GOMI Blog,* April 6, 2017. https://gomiblog.com/forums/healthy-living-bloggers/tone-it-up/page-135/.

peanbuttfing [pseud.]."I wanted to comment on this thread when it first popped up but I just have SO many thoughts it's hard to be concise...." *GOMI BLOG,* April 20, 2017. https://gomiblog.com/forums/healthy-living-bloggers/wandering-in-wellnesslauren-lives-healthy/.

reheated meat curai [pseud.]. "I have not been following her for long at all and only stumbled across her because of the..." *GOMI Blog,* April 29, 2017. https://gomiblog.com/forums/healthy-living-bloggers/wandering-in-wellnesslauren-lives-healthy/.

10 | Loving and Losing My Soulmate
The American Kennel Club, Inc. "Shih Tzu." *Dog Breeds.* Accessed 2022. https://www.akc.org/dog-breeds/shih-tzu/.

11 | Finally, A Diagnosis (Or Two)
Mayo Foundation for Medical Education and Research (MFMER). "Hashimoto's Disease." *Diseases & Conditions.* 2022. https://www.mayoclinic.org/diseases-conditions/hashimotos-disease/symptoms-causes/syc-20351855.

13 | Discovering Therapy

Meetup LLC. "About." *The Gloss: Portland.* Accessed 2022. https://www.meetup.com/gloss_portland/.

16 | In Loving Memory

Eamon & Bec. "For Lee." April 25, 2021. Video, 19:15. https://www.youtube.com/watch?v=N8VQEBQLBKI&t=140s.

Fitzgerald, Eamon, and Moroney, Rebecca. "Depression and Healing Through the Darkness with Lee MacMillan." March 1, 2021. REROOT with Eamon and Bec. Podcast, MP3 audio, 1:38:00. https://reroot.libsyn.com/embracing-change-and-healing-through-the-darkness-of-mental-health-with-lee.

speakupforlee [Lee MacMillan]. "My Mental Health Story." *Instagram*, December 5, 2020. https://www.instagram.com/tv/CIa9xDkBFKy/.

17 | Writing to Heal

Bartleson, Lauren. "A Letter to My Middle School Bully." *Medium, Behind the Facade,* April 10, 2021. https://medium.com/behind-the-facade/a-letter-to-my-middle-school-bully-62b26c8b210f.

18 | Behind the Facade

Bartleson, Lauren. "Behind the Facade." *Medium, Behind the Facade,* June 7, 2021. https://medium.com/behind-the-facade/why-is-talking-about-mental-health-still-taboo-b1e9c1a7af0d.

Bartleson, Lauren. "Why Is Talking about Mental Health Still Taboo?" *Medium, Behind the Facade,* May 19, 2021. https://medium.com/behind-the-facade/why-is-talking-about-mental-health-still-taboo-b1e9c1a7af0d.

21 | Writing *Insomnia*

Hodder, David. *Emotion and Feeling Wheel.* Accessed May 2022. Infographic. *Davidhodder.com,* resource.

MasterClass. "How to Write Haibun Poetry: Tips for Writing Poetry." *Writing.* September 3, 2021. https://www.masterclass.com/articles/how-to-write-haibun-poetry.

23 | Spiraling, Spiraling, Spiraling

Jewish Cemetery Association of Massachusetts. "Tattoos Allowed or Taboo?" *Jewish Cemetery, Burial and Mourning Customs.* 2022. https://www.jcam.org/Pages/Foundation/Education/articles/tattoos.php.

24 | Finding Meditation

Yoga with Adriene. "Meditation For Inner Peace—Yoga with Adriene." March 26, 2017. Video, 11:28. https://www.youtube.com/watch?v=d4S4twjeWTs.

25 | Lessons from Dad

United States Army. "Soldier's Creed." *Army Values.* Accessed May 2022. https://www.army.mil/values/soldiers.html.

United States Army. "The Army Values." *Army Values.* Accessed May 2022. https://www.army.mil/values/.

A Note on Statistics and Privilege

Bathla, Manish, Manpreet Singh, and Pankaj Relan. "Prevalence of Anxiety and Depressive Symptoms among Patients with Hypothyroidism." *Indian Journal of Endocrinology and Metabolism 20*, no. 4 (2016): 468–474. https://doi.org/10.4103/2230-8210.183476.

The Autoimmune Diseases Coordinating Committee. *Progress in Autoimmune Diseases Research.* US Department of Health and Human Services, 2005. Accessed June 12, 2022. https://www.niaid.nih.gov/sites/default/files/adccfinal.pdf.

Tips for Getting a Proper Diagnosis of an Autoimmune Disease. Eastpointe, MI: The American Autoimmune Related Disease Association, Accessed June 12, 2022. https://autoimmune.org/wp-content/uploads/2017/04/tips_for_auto_diagnosis.pdf.

To see a collection of photos and resources related to the book, visit laurenbartleson.com/memoir. You can also find the author on Twitter (@LaurenBartleson) and Goodreads (/LaurenBartleson). Thank you for following along!

CPSIA information can be obtained
at www.ICGtesting.com
Printed in the USA
LVHW020217071122
732502LV00003B/374

9 798885 045742